# How to Get
# a Headhunter
# to Call

# How to Get a Headhunter to Call

Howard S. Freedman

JOHN WILEY & SONS

New York • Chichester • Brisbane • Toronto • Singapore

*Library of Congress Cataloging in Publication Data:*

Freedman, Howard S. (Howard Samuel), 1941–
  How to get a headhunter to call.

    1. Executives—United States—Recruiting.  I. Title.
HD38.25.U6F74  1986      658.4'09      86-1604
ISBN 0-471-82844-0

Printed in the United States of America

10  9  8  7  6  5  4  3  2  1

*To my wife, Helen, for her loving support and editorial aid; to my former teacher, Jack Granofsky, for his support and guidance; and to my dad, Jack, who introduced his infant son to the library.*

# *Preface*

Several years ago, before executive search gained the notoriety and activity level that it now enjoys, I overheard a cocktail party conversation about the business. It was at the Darien, Connecticut home of a colleague. He and his family had just returned after a two-year assignment in Nigeria. His wife was showing neighbors the primitive, hand-carved statues they brought back as souvenirs. "Fascinating," said one gentleman. "They're marvelous," said a housewife. "And what does your husband do?" a woman inquired. "He's a headhunter," said the hostess matter-of-factly. The men nodded tentatively to themselves. The women looked at each other quizzically.

After nine years in executive search and after having interviewed thousands of executives, I realized that even though they all knew something about the business, they also lacked some vital information that could be useful in their career advancement. A few books have been written on the subject yet I sincerely believe that I have points to add. And, I felt I could present the material in a clear, straightforward fashion—this is the way it works, this is why, and, most importantly, this is how it can benefit you! The latter became my thrust.

The book specifically describes how to get a headhunter's attention, what to do thereafter—with him and major corporate clients. In a step-by-step approach, it walks an executive through the appropriate use of search. All the important current research is included.

A corporation wishing to use a headhunter's services is not neglected. There is material that will guide it in maximizing a working relationship with a search firm—enabling the best talent to be hired.

There are many "war stories" I've been privileged to personally experience or have colleagues and clients share from their experiences with headhunting. To me these humorous and informative vignettes are the joys of my labor.

Please note that the use of the male pronoun throughout the text is not intended as a sexist usage. Since he/she is awkward, the male pronoun is used to represent both genders.

HOWARD S. FREEDMAN

*New York*
*April 1986*

# Acknowledgments

I would like to thank the following Korn/Ferry International colleagues and business friends for their assistance: Virgil Baldi, Tony Barnes, Vince Brennan, Greg Coleman, Cathe Connors, Al Duarte, Debbie Erder, Dick Ferry, Frances Fisher, Stu Fishler, Duke Foster, Bill Gilbert, Mike Hazzard, Steve Israel, Lester Korn, Bob Kurtz, Alan Lafley, Bob Lo Presto, John McClement, Joe McMahon, Mercedes Mestre, Vince Morgan, Charlie Murphy, Bob Nesbit, Chuck Ollinger, Len Pfeiffer, Win Priem, Bill Reeves, Norm Roberts, Bob Rollo, Mike Rottblatt, John Schlueter, Nancy Streger, Bob Torok, Lee Van Leeuwen, Paul Verstraete, and Ron Woods.

H. S. F.

# Contents

# How to Get a Headhunter to Call

_____ SECTION 1 __

# Fundamental Facts

# CHAPTER 1

# What Is Executive Search?

The search consultant was seated next to a beautiful, dark haired, Latin American woman. By the time the plane was in the air and drinks were served, they were deep in conversation. Her English was weak; his Spanish was poor, but their eyes were dancing.

"What do you do?" she eventually asked.

"I'm retained by companies to find people who . . . "

"Oh, you're a collection agent?"

"No, I hunt senior people who . . . "

"Oh, you're with the CIA!"

"No, no, I'm paid in advance to search for talent who. . . . "

"Oh, why you no say so. You're a headhunter!"

---

Why does the executive search business exist? Aren't search firms just glorified employment agencies?

Search firms are often compared with agencies. This is one of the major misconceptions about the field. Retained search firms are not just contingency agencies working at a higher level. There are *major* differences.

## THE LEVELS AND TYPES OF POSITIONS RECRUITED FOR DIFFER

Retained search typically recruits at the very senior and upper-middle executive levels including board directors, chairmen and presidents through vice presidents and occasionally assistant vice presidents. Agencies generally place clerks, secretaries, and up through middle management. They occasionally overlap in the middle management area. Agencies and contingency firms don't handle the upper level assignments. Typical executive recruiting is in the $100,000 range, less often at lower salaries and frequently at $200,000 and considerably higher. Agencies work the teens through the $30,000 range with some contingency firms doing assignments into the upper teens. They infrequently see the level that is typical in the search business.

## EXECUTIVE SEARCH CONSULTANTS ARE PAID IN ADVANCE—WHETHER THEY FILL THE JOB OR NOT

Agencies are paid on delivery or contingent on a placement, and fees can go as high as 30 percent. The fees on some lower level jobs are borne by the candidate, not the employer.

Depending on the firm, search fees usually range between 25 and 35 percent of the executive's total compensation, including base and bonus, for the first year. Billing is in installments and the preponderance of the fee is typically paid in advance of the actual placement. Companies pay for the *search*.

Headhunters are on retainer and are paid whether they fill the position or not. They don't guarantee a placement, but ethical ones won't take on an assignment they believe isn't doable. Not wanting to lose a client or tarnish their reputations, they naturally persevere with difficult searches. Some searches, as a result, can take a year to complete. But the client may have been unsuccessful in all other recruiting endeavors and fully realizes the difficulty. The headhunter may make hundreds of calls before finding the needle in the haystack.

A major corporation in New Jersey asked a headhunter to find a vice president and manager for its southwest regional office in Houston, and insisted the person be a Texan. The position was challenging, but the compensation was inadequate. Knowing the market, the recruiter advised his client—a very good one—accordingly. Unable to increase the package yet having a strong need for a manager, the company urged the search firm to do the assignment even though the chances of success were slim. Not wanting to rebuff a client who gave him considerable business, the consultant accepted the search. Combing the Houston market over a three-month period, he developed five candidates. A senior vice president went to Houston to see them. He was stood up by one (rare at this level), another telephoned to say he'd changed his mind, and the others were deemed too inexperienced. The recruiter spent the next three months looking in Dallas for someone who could be relocated. Three candidates were developed, but the client wasn't interested and for different reasons: they knew the reputation of one fellow, another didn't have the extroversion they sought and the third man earned too much. The headhunter suggested searching in smaller Texas cities for someone who would have related, if not the exact, experience and who could be comfortable in a larger city. The next three months were spent hunting in cities like San Antonio, El Paso, Corpus Christi. One man was found in Dripping Springs.

He and the client met and liked each other. He was flown north to meet more senior management. He received an offer—much more than he was earning. By the end of the ninth month, he accepted. In the tenth month, shortly before he was to begin, he (and his wife) changed their minds. The charm and beauty of their small town and their fears about living in a big city were the reasons. During the eleventh and twelfth months, the head-hunter looked in vain for another candidate. The client even raised the dollars slightly. But not enough to lure anyone who was previously intrigued by the job, but found the money light. After two hundred calls and no success, the headhunter and the client agreed to stop the search.

## THE RECRUITING PROCESS IS DIFFERENT

Agencies usually fill positions by running advertisements aimed at attracting qualified people, or by drawing on their resume files. Executive search companies hardly ever run advertisements and only fill a small percentage of jobs using their files. Quality executive search companies also have automated resume retrieval systems serving domestic and international markets. Many executives don't look at advertisements and fewer respond to them. They fear circulating their resume to a blind box number advertisement or to an unknown individual running an advertisement—they don't know who else might see it, and whether this person is or knows their current employer. Besides, most senior positions aren't advertised and very senior ones never are. Of course, advertisements work. But they don't necessarily reach the targeted or best people for top executive positions. They reach those who are looking for a job change. In its ideal form, search goes after the stars in the field, the most suited to a particular position and not merely the job seekers.

Nearly all searches are completed by a headhunter calling executives who are performing the function their client needs a professional to cover. Search primarily serves the prospective employer and secondarily the candidate or submitter of a resume. The executive who is telephoned is very often not looking for a job change. He is approached, "cold-called," or hunted because he has the desired skills. He is wooed by an attractive executive position. Search goes after the gainfully employed. Many executives don't have a resume and most wouldn't deal with an agency. Search is the status, prestige way of changing jobs. The job comes after you. If you are an executive or a professional and good at what you do, word gets out and eventually you will be approached by a headhunter.

As an example of one process, a search for the president of a major leading company necessitated a headhunter teeing up appointments with presidents and executive vice presidents of several large leasing companies, financial institutions, and corporations in the United States and in the United Kingdom. Meetings were held in the recruiter's office, the executive's office, the recruiter's hotel suite or over breakfast, lunch, cocktails, or dinner at first-rate places. Traveling to the candidates over a seven-day period, the headhunter interviewed in New York, Chicago, Los Angeles, and London. Expenses ran several thousand dollars, but the client wanted the best.

Using search firms, and certainly prestigious ones, can enhance a company's recruiting effort, particularly when a small lesser-known or start-up operation uses their services. The flattered potential candidate who is called by a headhunter can quickly assess the seriousness of a prospective employer, since this company obviously thought enough of the post to go top of the line in recruiting for it (and to pay a big fee in advance). And when advertising, agencies and the old-boy network fail, executive search is an employer's court-of-last-resort.

With the latter point in mind, one wonders if the following position could have been filled in any way other than by using an executive search company.

---

The president of a company in El Salvador invited a headhunter down in order to find his replacement. He was leaving the firm because his life and his family's had been repeatedly threatened, and the director of public relations had been killed. Having met the recruiter at the airport, they traveled in an armored jeep to the executive's home, which was an armed camp, for a discussion. The president carried a pistol and had a larger weapon by the gearbox. They were followed by another armored carrier and guards. After staring intently at these other men, the headhunter asked the president, "Whose side are these guys really on?" "To tell the truth," said the president, "I don't really know."

---

## EXECUTIVE SEARCH CONSULTANTS ARE EXPERTS IN THEIR FIELDS

They are and generally were executives prior to entering the search profession. The partners and senior management in most firms grew up in another industry where they rose to the management ranks, often to vice president, executive vice president, or even president of a listed company. They learned a particular field very well and were known to senior people within it.

As a classic example, a vice president from one of the country's major banks retired at age 65, after more than 30 years of service, and as a second career joined the finance group of a giant executive search firm. Headhunters usually specialize or search in the fields from whence they came. Ten years later, he joined another prestigious search company, retiring in his eighties.

Typically, headhunters are college graduates and often hold advanced degrees. Their level of professionalism and experience is less frequently found among employment agency personnel. Executive search consultants are therefore better able to review the credentials of executives they interview—and they usually interview in-depth rather than screen. Specialization enhances evaluation skills. No candidate sees a client without being interviewed first.

Some employment agencies refer candidates to clients after having only seen their resumes or having talked to them on the telephone.

## EXECUTIVE SEARCH MAINTAINS A POTENTIAL CANDIDATE'S PRIVACY AND ANONYMITY

If after meeting with a consultant, the candidate decides not to pursue the position, his name is not mentioned to the client. Some agencies send resumes to companies without first alerting the would-be candidate. If a person registers with a few agencies, his resume could be multiply submitted to a company thereby making him seem too hungry or desperate for change. This would never happen in the search field because the candidate has to okay any referral of his credentials. Executive search is a highly confidential process.

A search consultant presented a candidate to the head of human resources. Impressed with him, he referred him to the line executive. Also favorably disposed, he bumped the man upstairs to his manager. This fellow recognized the executive's name. Four months earlier, an employment agency had sent an unsolicited copy of his resume for a different position. It had been returned with a note saying that they had no need for him.

The senior manager reluctantly met with this candidate—primarily because others thought he had ability. He thought the gentleman had shown poor judgment in registering with an agency and in allowing his resume to be circulated. However, he liked the candidate and hired him. But the man's leverage to negotiate a higher salary was weakened. The manager felt that he had been aggressively looking for a job—and had done it in a less than professional way.

## MANY EXECUTIVES HINDER THEIR CHANCES WITH BELOW-STANDARD RESUMES

Executive search firms write the resumes of all candidates whom they will present to a client, even if the individual has his own. They refine them, adding information relevant to the search in question and deleting the extraneous. Agencies generally do not have the time or expertise to do this. Headhunters often write personal evaluations too. They include information about a candidate that is legal, though usually not found in a resume, such as his appearance, attire, personality characteristics, style, and how he might fit in with the client and his executive team.


## HEADHUNTERS DO ALL THE WORK

A prospective employer may list a position with several agencies. He will, however, spend considerable time doing this, taking their inquiry calls regarding candidates and reviewing resumes. Similarly, if an employer runs an advertisement and gets over 100 replies, he has to wade through them, judging the abilities of unknown executives by their letters and resumes. If a search company is retained, they will serve up a few *qualified* candidates, thereby eliminating duplication and saving enormous amounts of time. Headhunters check references and put their findings in writing.


## THE MAJOR EXECUTIVE SEARCH COMPANIES ARE INTERNATIONAL IN SCOPE

They often operate several U.S. offices and many foreign branches. This network enables enormous recruiting capability. Recruiters can draw on the contacts of their colleagues, both near and far, to aid in locating or placing talented executives. Very few agencies even have a national presence.


## THE MAJOR EXECUTIVE SEARCH FIRMS USUALLY HAVE A RESEARCH STAFF

The staff can be sizable and located in many of the firm's offices around the United States and overseas. As college graduates and often librarians, they are trained in information gathering techniques. Using the guidelines and directions of headhunters as to which fields and companies, and what levels of executives to identify, researchers develop potential or target candidates' names (individuals who are usually working in competitive companies) whom the recruiter can call. How do they do this? They purchase specialized directories listing who's who in different fields. They may also have had the opportunity to look at staff directories of different companies that were lent to the headhunter by an executive who is an employee there or was an employee there whom he had hunted away. Additionally, magazines and newspapers in different fields are subscribed to and a reference library is maintained. A research staff reviews the search firm's resume files or computerized data bank to see if there are qualified people who match the job specifications. Many sophisticated search companies have computer linkage to other invaluable information services, such as Dun & Bradstreet (enabling quick information retrieval about numerous companies), *The Wall Street Journal,* *The New York Times* (all past articles from their morgues can be obtained), and so forth. Researchers telephone into companies and find out who holds a particular position. They have been known to visit an office building, peruse a lobby directory, and note which executive does what for a given company.

## EXECUTIVE SEARCH FIRMS MAY GUARANTEE A PLACEMENT FOR ONE YEAR

Agencies guarantee a placement for only one to three months. However, if a placement leaves a company of his own volition during the first year, some search firms replace the person without an additional hiring fee, except for minimal expenses (candidate or recruiter travel, resume preparation, etc.). Agencies don't offer such guarantees. They may prorate or return part of a fee if the person leaves before 90 days.

## HEADHUNTERS DON'T POACH
## IN THEIR OWN TERRITORY

Quality search companies don't hunt in a client company for candidates for other searches or clients. They keep out for as long as the relationship lasts. If after a year or two, depending on the search firm, no new business is forthcoming, the hands-off policy ends.


## SOME SEARCH COMPANIES HAVE A VENTURE
## CAPITAL ARM

Some search companies conduct searches for new ventures or start-up companies that need executives, but can't afford the services of a search firm. The recruiter may receive up to 50 percent of his fee in company stock.

For example, a small, new company may have spent the bulk of its budget on research and development. It now has a finished product, but lacks a marketing/sales person who can ably introduce it and get their message to the buying public. To meet his recruiting fee, the headhunter accepts partial payment in cash and the rest in stock. He gambles that the company will prosper, not fold as many do, and that the stock will eventually be salable at a price equivalent to or better than its original issuing value.

# CHAPTER 2

# Who Is Executive Search For?

If you're a disgruntled executive failing in your field, it's unlikely that you'll pick up the telephone one day and hear a headhunter at the other end. And, if you're an executive or a professional actively looking for a job change, approaching a search firm for help may not be the only answer.

The anomaly of the business is that while search consultants fill executive positions, it is generally with executives who, before they received the headhunter's call, were happy with their current jobs. In fact, headhunters primarily go after executives and professionals who are successful—but who might entertain changing positions if made aware of unusual opportunities. The headhunting philosophy is that any successful executive will probably at least listen to a new and unusual situation. Basically, that's how the business works. A telephone call, an offer too good to refuse, another "head" on the trophy board.

This is not to say that you can't be headhunted if you *are* looking for a job change. But in most cases, it is the recruiter who takes the initiative . . . and makes the first call. Headhunters work for client corporations. Using a position "spec" (specification), they set about looking for the right person to fill a spot.

At the low end, search is for executives in middle management generally earning $60,000 and up. Less work is done at this level, but it is the ground floor. The big firms and many high quality "boutiques" only do searches at the $80,000 level and *up*. They may occasionally accommodate a client and do an assignment at the $50,000 level, but it is rare.

Search is for those who have at least a few years' experience in a specific field and who are, generally, a few years out of college. But surprisingly, education is often not the most important factor. Many executives don't have university degrees, but their high incomes and sophisticated positions naturally put them in a headhunter's sights. Certain fields and professionals have a greater percentage of nondegreed executives—such as high-tech (it's new and evolving), operations (demonstrably so in banks), traders (particularly in foreign exchange and money markets), and so forth. This is also true of many executives from overseas—noticeably West Germany, Australia, and New Zealand—and in banking where many young men virtually apprentice out of high school. Senior level executive searches in these fields and professions usually require a degree in the United States, with a preference for an advanced one. However, in these and other professions, one can find individuals earning $100,000 and $200,000 annually who never went to college—and there are Americans among them.

As the chief executive officer (CEO) of a major investment bank put it, "When it comes to hiring successful traders, give me a street smart kid from the Bronx or Brooklyn over some Harvard MBA."

And well ensconced in the _Fortune_ magazine listing of America's richest few hundred is a near billionaire who not only never went to college, but in fact dropped out of high school in the tenth grade. His name is David Murdock and he is chairman of Pacific Holding Corporation, Cannon Mills Company, and Flexi-Van Corporation, director of KMI Continental Inc., a major real estate owner, and much more! He does, however, occasionally utilize search to find executive talent—even pedigree grads—for one or another of his companies.

Ivy League MBAs and certain professionals often begin careers at salaries above the search threshold. Despite this, they are rarely a match for the type of assignment search consultants get. They are usually recruited on-campus by corporations. A few years thereafter, they begin receiving calls from recruiters. Some investment bankers with three years of experience, atop an MBA and with a top house, can earn over $100,000 annually, while a five year veteran can earn over $200,000. And several make twice as much.

Search is for executives in all fields, although some are "hotter" than others, such as financial services and high-tech. In fact, big executive search firms have specialty groups serving major fields and industries.

Currently, executive search primarily serves white males. Fewer women and minorities are placed. There are many more white males who are senior executives, and consequently, there are more of them in the ponds headhunters fish in. However, times are changing. The sea of talent is broadening—through legislation, the human rights assertions of diverse minority groups, and their movement in increased numbers into the executive suite . . . motivated by aspiration, hard work, and ability.

Some searches are motivated by a company's desire to add minorities to an operation that may lack their beneficial input. Several years ago, the board of the Fireman's Fund was composed exclusively of men, all of whom were in their sixties or older. They wanted to add a well-known woman to the board. Shirley Temple Black got the job.

## EXECUTIVE SEARCH LESS FREQUENTLY SERVES CERTAIN GROUPS

### The Unemployed Executive

The attitude of most employees is, "If he's really top notch, why is he unemployed?" Granted there are thankful exceptions. To my mind comes the executive who inherited a new management either after an acquisition of his company or, as in a foreign bank, after the general manager completed his two- to three-year term and returned home. Suddenly a fine performer doesn't get along with his new leader or the management brings their own team with them. The executive may be given three, six, or more months' notice by management and then he is out. There are also a few independent souls who will leave a company and begin a full-time job search rather than suffer an unpleasant boss while simultaneously looking around. Despite good reasons for one's unemployment, it's a hurdle in the search world getting management to look at "beached" executives. And although recruiters have success in placing such individuals, the executive too often has to rely on his own contacts and efforts in locating a job. Nevertheless, this should not preclude contacting headhunters. However, if terminated "for cause" by your last company, chances of successfully being placed by a search firm are slim.

### Executives with Poor References

Most firms generally feel, "If he's any good, why are his references lousy?" Mitigating circumstances certainly have enabled headhunters to place executives who worked for companies or management whose reputations were themselves questionable; their client knew this and wasn't too biased. But when one's current reference is bad, the executive should be able to offset it with others—previous employers, clients, or executives who knew him professionally, if he wants a search firm's assistance.

## Average Performers

"If I wanted average, I wouldn't have retained your search services." Of course, some supposedly average executives at a Cadillac company may often look good or great to other slightly less prestigious firms. Put less harshly, there are executives rated average by their employers who have fine work records, educational backgrounds, and personal presence. One wonders if they wouldn't do better in a new and different environment which also seems more in keeping with their style, skills, and interests. A search firm's clients may occasionally make a business decision of this nature. But if you have an employment history of average to below average performance, it's very unlikely that a major search company can help you.

## Executives Whose Income Versus Their Age Ratio Reflects a Lag in the Former

"With all his experience, if he were any good, he'd be earning more." The executive rule is that you should earn more than your age. If you don't, it's rare that a headhunter will have a client with a need for your services. Somehow the barometer of the marketplace has evolved in this fashion. The low end $60,000 searches are generally filled by up-and-coming, young, middle management level executives. There are exceptions. A female executive, aged 55, was hunted from a $55,000 job to a $75,000 one. The new employer recognized the woman's ability and that women generally earn less than men doing a comparable job. Also, the lady had taken a 10-year leave of absence from her career to raise a family.

## Job Hoppers

People who have a series of short-term positions. "There must be something wrong with the guy if he keeps changing jobs so often." Employers wonder why the executive can't take root and progress in a company. It can't always be his employer's fault. So, after a handful of positions where each lasted two or three years, even with excellent and plausible reasons for departing (more money and a bigger job), an executive has gotten himself into some trouble. Search firms rarely are able to place people like this. These executives usually have to find the next assignment on their own.

Some fields, such as data processing and management information systems, have large numbers of people who leave after the project is completed. A prospective employer would still be wary of such individuals, but some search firms may be able to place them because the demand for their skills is high.

Why all these caveats? When prospective employers pay a search firm a hefty fee, they typically want the cream of the crop, and as they perceive them to be—unblemished! Their yardstick, fortunately, is not always rigid. Talent, personal chemistry, plausible reasons for circumstances, and the severity of any employer's need versus the availability of people, occasionally offset the demand for the perfect candidate. Sometimes a company isn't looking for Mr. Excellent because they can't afford him. Sometimes they aren't perfect themselves. This naturally gives a search firm more flexibility in considering candidates.

# CHAPTER 3

# How Executive Search Works— An Overview

The headhunter begins by making a new business call on a company to see if his services are needed, or he receives a call indicating a need—to fill a new post or to refill a vacant one. He then meets with the prospective client—one or more senior executives in the company—and develops particulars for a *job specification* (job spec). This consists of the position's title, whom it reports to, who reports to it, basic duties, an elaboration of responsibilities, candidate requirements, and compensation and benefits. The consultant also prepares a *contract* which may include information about the company, why the need exists, and information about the executive whom the new person will report to or work with. Some firms write a contract with a job spec as a portion of it. Contracts generally delineate the executive search company's background, how they do a search, and their fee arrangement for the assignment.


## RESEARCH

Once the contract is confirmed, the next phase of the search is *research*—developing the names of executives whom the headhunter can call regarding the job.

Related searches, previously completed by the headhunter and his colleagues, will be reviewed to see if a qualified person or source exists for *this* job. Colleagues are informed of the new search to see if they can recommend candidates or leads. Directories in selected fields are reviewed.

In addition to these basic techniques, researchers may also make telephone calls into companies (some occasionally use a phony line—pretext) in order to develop names. Ethics dictate that when a search firm calls into a company to find out, for example, who the director of marketing is, they do not disguise who they really are. Some firms may say they are a new magazine publisher and want to send a complimentary copy to the top marketing man (or some such story) and that they would therefore like his name. The search industry is beginning to develop stronger codes of ethics and these practices are decreasing, but slowly, because names are not given out easily. When a company realizes it's a search firm calling, they naturally keep quiet.

Consultants also call their contacts in the field to see whom they might know for the position. Networking is one of the great strengths of a search firm. Fundamentally, anyone can go to the library and look up a name and call that person, although some directories are not readily available to the public. But established contacts speed up the search process, enable a headhunter to zero in on high quality and possibly interested executives, and to reach these busy people because the recruiter comes with an introduction. Sometimes the right person may be in an unsuspected place—he may have left his original field and want to return—and it's networking that puts a recruiter on to him. However, networking can often have interesting psychological aspects. Sometimes the headhunter's contacts, who are called as sources, decide *they* are interested. Telling them the situation isn't right or a match for their experience—without ruffling feathers—is delicate work. Occasionally contacts say they know a perfect candidate, but he's on their staff and they don't want to lose him. The headhunter must then decide if the friendship exceeds his need. Executives have been known to recommend, in strict confidence, a rival such as their manager or a strong peer!

## TELEPHONE CALLS

Armed with the names of potentially appropriate executives, *the consultant begins his calls*—presenting the search situation on each occasion. He might begin with, "My name is Mr. Search from Headhunter's, Inc. I'm working on a search to locate a senior vice president of marketing for a major financial services company in New York. I wondered if you would be interested in hearing some details about it?"

He usually doesn't give the client's name because most don't want it known that they are looking for a key person until an interested, potential candidate is face-to-face with the recruiter. Basic, relevant information is provided about the position and the company—enough to ideally whet the appetite and create some mystique.

If they are not interested or suitable, he will treat them as "sources" or leads to other possible candidates—asking them about people they know with similar backgrounds who might care to hear of a new position. (The consultant may even hear about other search needs since he is gaining intelligence regarding the marketplace with each conversation.)

It can sometimes take 50 to 75 telephone conversations in order to develop five potential candidates worth interviewing. A very tough search may require contacts and discussions with over 100 or even 200 professionals. And most executives are not reached on the first telephone call.

## INTERVIEWS

When an interested party is developed through a telephone conversation, the search consultant then screens and determines qualifications. The initial mutual exchange of information is a prelude to *an interview*. The consultant will then meet with the candidate, identify the client, explain the assignment in greater detail, and if the executive is still interested, interview him and determine his eligibility. If qualified, the headhunter prepares a resume for the executive. Resumes are generally two to three pages long.

About three to four weeks from the time the headhunter's search contract was signed, he usually visits the client with the resumes of a few qualified people. He may have from three to five candidates to discuss. Some headhunters send candidates for interviews as they develop them. Out-of-town candidates are presented in abridged resume form based on notes taken over the telephone. If the client is interested, the recruiter then either travels to the executives or flies them in for follow-up discussions.

The prospective *employer* typically *meets* with two or three *candidates,* inviting back one or two. A few clients need to see five or more candidates before they can focus in on the ideal one. The selected one or two semifinalists meet other executives in the company on subsequent visits. As a middleman, the headhunter is consulted by the client and candidates, both questioning him about the attitudes and reactions of the other.

## NEGOTIATIONS

A finalist emerges; an *offer* is made and the consultant often negotiates the differences on both sides until a "hire" occurs. Sometimes a candidate wants the job, but the compensation package isn't enough. He may, for example, want a larger base salary. The employer may not be able to accommodate this because he has people in equal or similar assignments who earn less. The headhunter may propose an up front, one time bonus which gives the candidate the dollars sought while circumventing salary constraints. Or, the consultant may propose a salary review in six months, instead of the typical annual one.

Perhaps a candidate wants more responsibility than the prospective employer is offering. A consultant may propose that the additional duties be given by year end, and management may be willing to do so. But suppose the final candidate wants a guarantee that he will be given the added authority, and that it happen now, not later. The headhunter may try to cut a deal whereby the company gives the executive these desired responsibilities within three to six months—as soon as he grows comfortable and demonstrates competence with these other tasks.

The newly hired executive then gives *notice* to his current employer. He usually does this by informing his manager that he has accepted another position and that he'd like to leave in two weeks (usually), or three or four. The time hinges on how long he has been with his employer, the level of his position, and what straits he puts them in by a sudden or premature departure. Responsible senior executives leave when it's convenient for their old firm, without, naturally, hurting the new arrangement.

## FINALE

Next comes *reference checking*—an important step. Occasionally, this is done before an offer is made. It's a sensitive issue that is best accomplished afterwards. Offers are made contingent on satisfactory references. So it behooves the executive to be candid about them.

Sometimes the candidate accepts a position, gives notice to his employer, but gets an attractive *counter-offer* and decides to stay where he is. The consultant may try to reactivate the number two and number three candidates, if there are any, or be forced to begin the search again—at no additional fee.

The newly hired executive and the headhunter have forged a business relationship. It's the kind of relationship that may continue to benefit each of them in various ways over the years to come.

# CHAPTER 4

# An Inside Look at Search Firms and Their Consultants

The more an executive knows about headhunters, the more effectively he can deal with them and maximize the service they provide.

## LARGE VERSUS SMALL

Executive search firms come in large, medium, and small sizes—from hundreds of employees in dozens of locations to a one-man office. Some offer only domestic assistance, others have international capabilities. Some have a general practice serving many fields and types of positions while others are specialists. What are the advantages and disadvantages of using one or the other from the perspective of the executive?

If search firms service your field, then they are of use to you regardless of size. The large firms have more clients and do more searches at different levels and in more locations—obviously a plus. Quality resumes often circulate, sometimes in a summary sheet form, around their system making staff aware of you. If you are willing to relocate, a resume sent to a firm with multiple offices may attract the attention of recruiters in other cities—more bang for your effort. If you want to send out only a few resumes, that is, initially make contact with only a few search firms—you are likely to get more action from a big firm. Of course, there are small executive search companies with some of the same clients and other quality corporate relationships of their own. However, many small firms do not retain mail-in resumes.

If you are receptive to international placement, the large search companies with overseas offices are better for you.

As an accommodation to a client, a recruiter can, for instance, arrange for a multilingual U.S. executive to interview with consultants in the firm's London, Brussels, Paris, and Frankfurt offices.

This is what happened in the case of an executive in New York City who asked his headhunter friend if he could aid his son-in-law (an American aerospace engineer living in Paris) in finding another job, possibly in the United States. The headhunter, with the consent of this gentleman, showed copies of the resume to the heads of both the international and aerospace departments of his firm in New York, and also sent copies to his London and Paris offices. In this way, the candidate, who was willing to settle wherever the job required, had the field covered through the efforts of a single firm.

If you know a specialty search firm that has placed people in your field in attractive positions and with good companies, they are clearly of value to you. However, the large search firms have equal, if not stronger, track records and capabilities. Many have several specialty desks serving different fields within the context of their general practice. It is not uncommon to have all of the hot fields and hot jobs represented. So you will find search consultants covering financial services, high-tech, consumer products, retail/merchandising, real estate, and so forth. Their offices are adjacent and these men and women exchange ideas and talk about their work. Lists of new search assignments also circulate. Often a talent scout in one field abets his neighbor in another with a recommendation. As a result, a general manager or perhaps a financial services or MIS (management information systems) executive crosses industry lines to an opportunity. Could this happen as easily in a small or specialty firm?

A billion dollar company with a worldwide operation was searching for a new president. They wanted someone from outside their industry because they didn't respect those whom they knew in top posts within it. The requirements included: general management experience with large staffs located in numerous places, international business experience, a financial background, and an impeccable demeanor. By consulting with his colleagues in various fields, the headhunter was able to draw on the specialized knowledge of each of find candidates to recommend— and eventually place.

## THE HIERARCHY AND STRUCTURE IN A SEARCH FIRM

What is the typical hierarchy and structure in an executive search firm? There is either a chairman or president; large search firms may have both. Beneath them are key executives whose prime responsibility is new business development and account management. Their titles include vice president, consultant, director, principal, partner, or more exalted variations (managing director, executive vice president, senior vice president, senior partner, etc.). The titles are bestowed on those who bring in a lot of new business or manage other officers. There is no uniformity of titles. One may even find the head of a particular specialty division occasionally titled chairman of the XYZ practice. Very large companies may have regional directors over a cluster of offices. But regardless of titles, nearly all officers are charged with bringing in business and managing accounts (directly or indirectly). Giant firms may have a board of directors traditionally composed of a few senior executives from within the firm and outside directors. Large and medium size firms often have an executive committee primarily composed of senior management from within the company. And some companies have levels of associates who work for a partner and with his direction, often make the voluminous cold calls trying to develop candidates. This is also done by all levels of executives, though senior management usually calls their network of contacts. Many associates have accounts of their own and are moving towards the senior ranks. Entrance to officer level generally hinges on developing a minimum amount of new business. Some firms also put a premium on filling jobs. There are also research staff who develop the names of executives in the companies to be hunted in.

## THE BACKGROUNDS
## OF EXECUTIVE SEARCH CONSULTANTS

In quality firms, the partners generally held executive positions prior to entering the search business. Many are specialists who practice search serving their former industry. A few have grown or developed within the ranks of this newer field, having started as an assistant to a consultant, progressing upward as they learned the business.

There is a tendency for headhunters to have expertise in one or a few fields, whether gained from having been in them or over a period of time in the search business. Why? The growing complexity and the uniqueness of each hot field and hot job require that they know enough about them to "talk" the business with prospective clients and candidates. Companies rarely pay large fees in advance unless they have confidence that the headhunter knows the industry he will search in. There are exceptions, however; sometimes clients have enough general confidence in a headhunter to give him the assignment.

Educationally, the professional staffs in top firms are usually college graduates, often with advanced degrees, including MBAs, LLBs, and even PhDs, and from leading schools.

There are a few women in the upper ranks in several of the major firms; their numbers are increasing, but are still disproportionate. There are, however, many female professionals in the tiers below, and many get promoted. A few have made it to the partnership level. Where other minority groups are concerned, the big international firms have professional staffs around the world who are of diverse nationalities. Hispanic and black representation in the United States is meager. Some women and blacks have formed their own smaller, often specialty firms.

At the partner level, headhunters tend to be in their mid-thirties and up—the preponderance being older. To first become successful in another field takes time. Consultants also need experience and maturity which enable them to more effectively interface with the senior management of diverse companies. The professional ranks, below senior management, are primarily filled with younger staff although there are many who are in their forties and up.

## HOW AND WHY DID HEADHUNTERS GET INTO THE BUSINESS?

A few were reverse recruited. That is, they were called by a head-hunter to discuss a position with a client and the conversation eventually turned, whether from their initiation or the recruiter's, to the search field and eventually to the possibility of their joining the company. Others were specifically approached, since they were well regarded executives in their particular industries, as to whether they would like to apply their backgrounds to the search business. Still others, after a first or subsequent encounter with a recruiter, had a seed planted. They experienced the occupation as a candidate and liked what they saw. This germinated over time to a real interest and they may have started contacting search companies seeking more information and possible employment.

The search field is relatively new—perhaps a tad over 40 years old—and exciting in its early adulthood transition, growth, and development. No doubt executives sensed opportunity here, and less bureaucracy and structure than their large corporate environments may have burdened them with. So hunting heads became a challenge and an interesting new career option that also enabled the use of expertise acquired over a period of years in their former endeavors.

## WHAT ARE THE PERSONALITIES AND STYLES OF HEADHUNTERS?

Since they come from many fields and careers, they vary widely. Yet senior management have certain qualities which differentiate them.

They are usually *independent minded*. They have their own client relationships and work in a one-to-one fashion with them. Subordinates take their direction from officers so a search is not a team effort of peers. The associates who move up in a search firm demonstrate the ability to develop their own business (new searches and clients) and to fill them (by themselves or by orchestrating others).

By virtue of the nature of the search business, headhunters are *transaction oriented*. Each new search is a start-up situation that puts their reputation on the line. Filling the job is expected by the client (they paid in advance for the service); failure is always possible (perhaps a final candidate can't be found). Although relationships and repeat business develop, the recruiter rarely works with his many placements in an ongoing hand-in-glove fashion. When he finishes a search, he is on to the next one. Contact is loosely maintained with the executive placed. He may do an occasional search for that person, more often for his company, but the process makes him an outside consultant rather than a staff or team member.

Good headhunters are people who are able to *cope with pressure,* that is, juggling several ongoing searches simultaneously, trying to quickly find high-caliber candidates, and maintaining amicable business dealings with diverse clients who often want Mr. Right yesterday.

One headhunter left for a prearranged four day seminar just at the point when negotiations between his final candidate and a Japanese client were heating up. There was a need to be in frequent communication with both parties, but it was difficult. He was ensconced in a classroom from 7:30 A.M. to 6:30 P.M. with infrequent 10 minute breaks and one hour for lunch. To complicate matters, the only nearby telephone was deliberately placed on a wall in the lavatory to discourage calls. When he called his secretary to check up on messages, he was told about his client's recent panic call and urgent need to speak with him—the candidate was having second thoughts. He spent the next 40 minutes standing at the wall telephone in the men's room, speaking slowly to his client, listening attentively because of the client's accent and limited English, and relaying back and forth between him and the candidate. All of this in the men's room while "business as usual" went on around him. Talk about stress!

Headhunters do everything that you would expect in order to cope with pressure, from various forms of exercise (mostly white-collar oriented—tennis, squash, golf, and jogging) to smoking, drinking, and overeating.

One took a course that could have been dangerous. When this headhunter's new secretary knocked on his closed door, no one answered. So she opened it (barely missing his head) and stepped into the office (barely missing his head). There he lay on the floor—flat on his back, in a trance, meditating.

They are *gregarious* and *social minded* individuals who enjoy working with quality people to find more quality people for their client companies. The headhunter's profile is part consultant plus a dab of psychologist and a dash of salesman.

There is a *competitive nature* to a good headhunter. He is not always handed a search, but often competes with a few rival executive search companies to obtain the assignment. The recruiter may call on or be called in by the director of human resources or a senior line manager to discuss the company's need. He would then display his knowledge in the area of their need, his credentials, his firm's, and so forth.

They are *persistent.* As previously stated, it can take 50 to 100 or more telephone calls to executives to develop a few qualified and interested ones—and they're not often reached on the first attempt. In its business development phase, obtaining a search is not unlike any marketing and sales effort. Headhunters mail letters or literature about themselves and their companies to prospects. It isn't unreasonable for new consultants to make 100 calls and mail 100 letters (or more or both) before connecting with a company with a need or an interest in discussing it with them.

Headhunters are *hard working* and *ambitious.* They often meet candidates for 7:30 A.M. or 8 A.M. breakfasts and then may have a dinner interview at the end of the day. Busy executives often don't have the time to explore new job opportunities in the 9 A.M. to 5 P.M. time frame. So executive search consultants have to make themselves available in order to hook up with high powered achievers whom they typically pursue.

"Neither wind, nor rain, nor sleet, nor hail . . . "; the mailman cannot compare to this particular headhunter. He got in his four-wheel-drive jeep and drove from New York City to Providence, Rhode Island in a near blinding snow storm, through closed highways, to secure a search with a new client.

## WHAT MOTIVATES EXECUTIVE SEARCH PEOPLE?

Money motivates and therefore so does *new business* from either a preexisting client or a new one. And new business is developed in many ways. Headhunters may invite prospects to dine in order to get better acquainted. They also socialize at select clubs and gatherings where they can meet influential people who may retain them or introduce them to someone who can. Even the executive who doesn't get the job has been known to use the recruiter because he was impressed with the way he operated— a flattering occurrence. Candidates are all potential clients. Headhunters lecture, publish, review periodicals in their field looking for ideas, are active in professional organizations, and very infrequently answer a "blue bird" call (a company calls them with a search need). Searches have been given out on golf courses, tennis courts, in first class airplane seats, by conducting wine tasting seminars, and of course, by making voluminous cold calls via the telephone.

Another motivant is *filling positions* and doing good work, that is, finding the best candidates or those who meet the client's wishes.

The previously mentioned dynamisms give headhunters the desired *prestige* and *power* among clients, peers, subordinates, and the general public which spurs them on to continued efforts.

Consultants enjoy meeting different and interesting *people* who are typically above average in intelligence and success—if not occasionally very human and vulnerable, and who find unusual ways of coping with extraordinary situations. For example, there was a Jewish economist who was offered a position with a West German bank. His in-laws, however, had lost family in the concentration camps, and he was sensitive enough to ask them whether it would upset them for him to accept. They said "no," so he said "yes."

There are no stereotypes, and headhunters encounter highly successful business people with overt or covert idiosyncracies.

---

An executive was to be flown in a company plane from his home in Cleveland to New York City to meet the search committee of a prospective new employer's board. Shortly before his arrival time, the headhunter received the following call. "I'm sorry, but I can't come. I thought I could get up the courage to get on the plane given the circumstances. But I can't overcome my fear of flying. The only way I can come is if I take my wife with me for support . . . and if I also have a few pops on the flight." This made both the candidate and the headhunter look bad in the eyes of the board—the candidate was dropped. The consultant later referred him to another client who was understanding and more concerned with the man's achievements than his phobias.

Another example was when a headhunter placed a gifted and successful executive who used to suffer with manic-depressive bouts, but whose use of a stabilizing drug has prevented his ailment from interfering with his career.

Working on *new* and *varied assignments* stimulates and challenges search consultants.

A former Special Forces officer, now a headhunter, received a call from a former CIA executive. "I want to retain your services. I need 12 men. They must be experts in light weapons, United States and foreign, as well as hand-to-hand combat. The group must include a pilot, a navigator, a communications expert, and a medic. The boys must be in good shape and be 10 or more years out of the service. Can you do it?"

"What's their mission?"

"They're going to go into a Third-World country. It's a one month job. The pay is $100,000 tax free for each man."

The headhunter calculated the fee—$30,000 for each man or $360,000. Although he knew he could deliver, he was skeptical about the effect on his firm's reputation if they fulfilled this request. He brought the proposal to his senior management. They agreed with him and turned it down.

Headhunters enjoy elegant dining and travel although both are so tied to business dealings that they can't always enjoy them to the hilt. In fact, in terms of eating the consultant must develop self-discipline, exercise regularly, or get fat.

A headhunter spent a few days in Chicago and Los Angeles interviewing candidates over breakfast, lunch, and dinner—in top restaurants. His wife and children were jealous. His parents were proud. His in-laws thought he was a big shot. But when he returned home from the trip, he took two Alka-Seltzers and went straight to bed.

## WHAT DO HEADHUNTERS EARN?

They are typically paid a salary plus a bonus. Depending on the size of the executive search firm, an estimate of a partner's total annual earnings may range from 25 to 50 percent of the fees which he generates. Typically, the larger the percentage paid to the recruiter, the smaller the firm. Why? Big executive search companies with established names and public relations assistance enable headhunters to do more business. The headhunter pays dues by getting a smaller percentage of a bigger pie. This doesn't mean that one headhunter earns more than the next. In general, partners earn about $75,000 to well in excess of $300,000 in some instances. The $100,000 plus level is not uncommon. Salaries range from about $50,000 to the $200,000 level. Of course, the founding partners earn much larger undisclosed sums.

The nonpartner, professional staff earn from $25,000 to approximately $75,000. Base salaries start in the $20,000s and range to the $60,000s. Bonuses make up the difference.

Other nonsalaried compensation may include a 401K (a tax shelter where you usually put aside a percentage of your salary and the company matches all or part of it), diverse investment programs, stock options, profit sharing, and so forth. Perks are often provided that may include a car or car allowance, clubs, an expense account, special health benefits, and so forth.

# SECTION II

# Executive Essentials

# CHAPTER 5

# Getting the Headhunter's Attention— Part One

According to *The AESC News Report* (the publication of the Association of Executive Search Consultants, an organization composed of many search companies), "There were less than ten significant firms in our business in 1959." Today it is "an industry which produces revenues in the nine figure area."

*Executive Recruiter News* presents a still brighter picture. It notes that search is a $1.5 billion annual industry with revenues evenly divided between retained search (fees paid in advance) and contingency firms (fees paid on delivery of a placement). There are more than 1500 search firms in the United States and they employ some 10,000 recruiters. The industry places about

80,000 executives yearly with an average annual salary of $50,000. And industry experts see these numbers increasing.

For each executive placed, three to five are typically presented to a company and it is not uncommon for 50 or more to have been approached as prospective candidates. Therefore, each year some 320,000 executives interview with headhunters and possible clients, while approximately 4 million prospective candidates receive telephone calls from recruiters. So there is an enormous amount of activity in the field.

And the executive ranks are expanding. Companies are hiring executives at a vigorous rate and demand for senior managers earning $100,000 or more annually continues to escalate, according to the *Quarterly National Index of Executive Vacancies.* The *Index* is based on a quarterly survey of 750 Korn/Ferry International clients who are among the nation's largest corporations and nonprofit organizations, including government agencies, universities, and cultural institutions. The Index records the hiring of executives earning $100,000 or more annually.

Given the dramatic increase in the number of executive search firms, the millions of executives who are approached by them, and the huge and continuing growth in the executive ranks, it is not so much a question of how to get a headhunter to call, but rather how to get a headhunter to call you, more often and with the right position. There are several ways an executive can draw a headhunter's attention.

## BE SUCCESSFUL AT WHAT YOU DO

What does this mean? Simply stated, if you are a middle manager in a company that has a dozen like you, then you should enjoy more power, prestige, and be one of the best—in terms of management, peer, customer, and your industry's evaluation of you. And you should be among the highest paid. If you are in the top spot in your specialty within your company, the aforementioned basically holds true with an emphasis that you be perceived within your industry as one of the best. When headhunters network among their contacts, they are usually looking for leads that will direct them to just such people.

A multibillion-dollar company was in the market for a head auditor. They were prepared to compensate the ideal candidate well beyond market standards in order to attract the best. Money not being the sole factor which would entice a successful executive, the company also presented an attractive career path. The recruiter, who had previously done search work in this and related fields, contacted his business friends in corporations, Big 8 accounting firms, and banks—inquiring about the exceptional auditors they knew. A list of 23 people was targeted. The recruiter mentioned them to his client who eliminated six names— he either didn't respect the audit function within their company or knew of the person and wasn't interested. Of the 17 remaining, all were satisfied with their jobs and were well taken care of by their employers. To entice one away ultimately required a large sign-on bonus (not limited to the world of sports) and a six-figure, interest-free mortgage loan.

Occasionally an enlightened management will recommend one of its stars because it reflects back positively on them and the company, and they are partial to seeing this individual advance. What the recruiter may hear is, "I'd hate like hell to lose him because he's so darn good, but an opportunity like you're describing won't develop here for some time. So why not give the best man a shot at it."

There are innumerable, diverse, and even subtle elements and influences that enable one to become successful. And among the major studies which have addressed the issue, a few were done by search firms.

*Korn/Ferry International's Executive Profile: A Survey of Corporate Leaders,* produced in conjunction with the Graduate School of Management at UCLA, is a prime example. It represents interviews with 1708 senior executives (executive vice presidents to vice presidents in different functions) from the Fortune 500, including commercial banking, life insurance, diversified financial, retailing, and transportation companies. Four thousand diverse executives were approached to obtain this sample which was ultimately a predominately white male, Protestant population with an average age of 53. The study indicates that executive men believe the single most significant factor in bringing about success is *hard work*. Second comes ambition, drive, and the desire to achieve. Women executives agree, but reverse the order.

The need to achieve coupled with strong interpersonal skills were deemed key reasons for CEO success in an American Management Association survey report, conducted by Professors Charles Margerison and Andrew Kakabadse, entitled *How American Chief Executives Succeed*. They surveyed 700 CEOs to obtain these results.

Heidrick and Struggles (another major search firm) developed a *Portrait of a CEO* which showed that 60 percent of those studied spend as many as 60 hours weekly at work, and they have insufficient time with their families and outside interests. However, they also enjoy work more than others. The study was based on a survey of over 300 diverse CEOs from major industrial and nonindustrial corporations.

The Heidrick and Struggles *Mobile Manager* study, which had nearly 800 executive respondents including vice presidents through chairmen, showed that leadership ability was rated the most important factor in upward mobility by two-thirds of the respondents. The second most important consideration was a record of success. Hard work and results were tied for third; intelligence wasn't far behind though in fourth place. Further down in fifth place was supportive superiors although most executives had them.

The value of career planning also emerges when the backgrounds of senior executives are reviewed—what school to attend, what to study, where and at what to work . . . ?

## WORK IN A HOT JOB AND IN A HOT FIELD OR INDUSTRY

Naturally, what is hot isn't always so, but some areas have greater consistency. The cool endeavors periodically warm up, although they always have executive recruiting needs. With differing frequencies both have enabled accession to more senior positions. In Korn/Ferry International's study:

> *When asked which functional area he believes currently provides the fastest route to the top in his company, our corporate respondent and his peers mentioned finance/accounting, marketing/sales and general management. Few see personnel, production, the professional/technical or international areas as providing a "fast track." As to a future fast track "route to the top," our corporate respondent and his peers continue to favor finance/accounting, were less confident of the marketing/sales route, and more confident of the general management route. A few of his peers cautiously predict, however, that the professional/technical area, and possibly the international area, may be the future fast routes to senior-level management.*

*The Chief Executive Background and Attitude Profiles,* by Arthur Young & Company's search arm, surveyed 800 top business leaders in various fields and found similar results. "The most promising path to the top corporate office is through general management." But other routes include finance, law, technology, operations, and marketing/sales.

Heidrick and Struggles' *CEO* study found the route to the top to be first via sales/marketing and then finance/accounting, manufacturing/operations, engineering, research, and legal.

*Korn/Ferry International's Profile of Women Senior Executives,* developed with UCLA, was designed to yield a profile of women executives that would contrast similarities and differences, as well as compare them with the previous male group. The sample population consisted of Fortune 1000 firms and included all the earlier job titles and functions in addition to presidents, chief executive officers, and chief operating officers. Six hundred names were developed and 300 women responded. The typical female senior executive was a white Protestant with an average age of 46. Women senior executives considered the fastest "route to the top" for women to be the fields of marketing/sales, financial/accounting, and professional/technical. They felt the fastest route for men was marketing/sales, financial/accounting, and general management—the same assessment the male executives made. Down the line, female executives believed general management would be of increased importance to both women and men. As the careers of women executives progressed, "There was a significant trend towards becoming generalists instead of functional experts (a tendency also noted among male executives)."

The positions which *are* hot in the marketplace in which the aforementioned senior executives obviously call the tune, are perhaps no surprise, and are revealed in the *National Index of Executive Vacancies*. It showed that the most sought after executives are, in order, general managers, marketing/sales, financial people and then production/manufacturing/engineering executives.

The search for executive talent is ongoing in good and bad times. When the target is general managers, marketing and sales people, it connotes a strengthening economy and optimism, expansion within a company, and a desire to take advantage of higher sales. When the economy sours, the need is for financial executives who can ideally solve a company's money problems and cut costs.

The hottest field/industry over the last several years and one that continues to hire aggressively is *financial services* (banking, investment banking, insurance, and brokerage), which recruits more diverse executives and in the greatest numbers. It has accounted for one-fifth to one-quarter of the total executive market demand for many years. Why? Nationwide banking has created jobs across state lines. Deregulation has enabled banks, investment banks, brokerage firms, and insurance companies to enter into one another's business, creating new needs in these institutions as they become more alike.

There has been a strong and persistent need for commercial bankers and in particular lending officers. Some industry experts see the trend cooling in the future and predict the emergence of commercial paper issuers. Investment banker needs are high especially in the merger and acquisitions area. The capital markets are hot—in Eurocurrency transactions and in interest rate swaps—and merchant bankers with these skills are in demand.

Portfolio managers and research analysts are sought after because of their abilities to add value to the investment process. An increased need has developed for financial planners who advise companies and individuals on investing. It is viewed as a young profession, less than 20 years old, whose professional ranks have tripled to close to 20,000 in the last several years (judging from the membership of the International Association of Financial Planners). *The New York Times Financial Planning Guide* cites this "growing body of professionals" as even larger in number. The need for management information systems as well as data processing executives in financial services will continue over the next several years. Financial services has and will continue to hire many chief executive officers and chief operating officers.

Demand for *high technology* executives is second only to financial services—and it's growing. The need is primarily for general managers with technical skills. Small start-up companies, in particular, need management with good profit and loss skills acquired at larger companies. It's hard to find these people; everyone wants them. One's promotional route is often from a key technical position into a general management role, such as running a division. Then, perhaps with the assistance of a headhunter, one can become a chief operating officer in a modest-sized technical company.

Talented marketing people are also hot. They are the visionaries and strategic planners who can find out the needs in the marketplace and relay them to the engineers. Manufacturing executives are in demand. More sophisticated ones are needed who have cost reduction savvy. Engineers and financial specialists are also sought after.

Telecommunications is the hottest growth area. This includes start-ups and companies building their own communications networks to bypass an AT&T. It also means hardware and software development. The marriage of the telephone and the computer is playing a role in the development of office and home systems of the future (shop and pay bills by using your computer).

The field of artificial intelligence is growing in the decision support area. Financial services is a first frontier for artificial intelligence. Robotics is another arm of artificial intelligence. It's strong in factories where robots are increasingly used to avoid human error.

Medical electronics instrumentation (computers and electronics paired with health care) is quite dynamic. Doctors use these new tools to speed up data gathering and to diagnose faster.

The personal computer will remain busy although the shake-out in the industry will leave only a few giant survivors (IBM, Tandy, etc.).

The *defense industry* was, is, and will continue to be hot. The leading edge of technology often finds its first application in defense. Highly engineered product areas need executives. The hottest areas are: star wars, communications, command and control, and missiles and space. The manufacturing process, which is changing, needs financial planners and financial managers.

After a period of heavy acquisitions, the *real estate* field's hot jobs are property and asset management. They need people who can manage income producing real estate. There is long-term growth and stability in this area. It is not viewed as flashy and exciting, but everybody wants these people. Also hot are chief financial officers—people with control skills.

The *consumer products* industry is busy in companies making computers and in the packaged goods area. But for the field to become really hot again, exciting new products are needed. The lustre is presently off and will remain so for a while. However, marketing people are needed and this need will continue. It's a positive sign; control executives are needed in bad times, and corporate planners are needed to develop new products.

In the *merchandising and retail* field, the hot areas are in chains—women's ready-to-wear specialties, catalog/mail order, electronics, and toys. All are perceived by experts as offering long-term growth with the exception of the toy chains which are seen as short term. Specialty stores have grown rapidly without developing sufficient internal talent—hence their needs.

There are four functional areas where demand is keen and will persist. One is merchandising, for a person who can predict or create the fashion market. Someone who can look at a line of (European) products and adapt them for another (U.S.) market. It may be someone who can direct the designer. The needs exist on the apparel, manufacturing, and retail sides of the business.

Another talent is salespeople—they know the decision makers and have the contacts. They introduce top management to good products that sell. This need exists on the apparel and manufacturing sides of the business.

Companies may give the merchandiser and the salesman a good administrative or financial type to work with them. They walk behind the creative or selling geniuses, keeping them in check and acting as confidants.

Store operations managers are gaining in popularity in the specialty chains. They can run hundreds of units in numerous states, know how to display the merchandise in a store, and have strong people skills.

The *health services* field is actively recruiting. Why? Third-party payers (the government, Medicare, etc.) want to reduce the amount of money they are laying out for reimbursement. This has exerted pressure to change the way the system operates. It has created a need for a different kind of hospital manager. *Hospitals* reported a trend in the need for managers with for-profit business experience. There are few such senior executives in the health care field with this background. Hence, these executives are recruited from for-profit companies for both nonprofit and for-profit hospitals, and they come from diverse disciplines.

Other trends include the continued development of hospital chains, for-profit and nonprofit. Also, specialty services are expanding—food services, kidney dialysis, and so forth—and each can be run as a business. Hot jobs further include: financial executives, planners, chief executive officers, directors of acquisitions and business development, administrators, consultants (for health services consulting firms), and marketing people.

In the *public and education* sectors, the hot jobs are those that increase revenues or raise funds—for community, educational, health care, cultural institutions, and the arts. In the public area, these executives are called economic development specialists; in education and nonprofit institutions, they are referred to as development directors. Data processing people are needed in both. Also, people who can run enterprises and manage the bottom line are sought. They are corporate-type public servants, and they run hospitals, airports, harbors, utilities, and so forth. These needs will continue over the next few years.

There has been increased executive hiring in the *leisure and entertainment* industry. The need is for general managers with financial and marketing backgrounds for the pay TV and cable fields. The reason is that an upsurge in the economy has created an increased demand in the industry. Hiring is often from other fields, such as consumer electronics firms. Why? These newer entertainment enterprises haven't had sufficient time to grow their own talent.

Similarly, the *leisure and hotel* field is hot because Americans increasingly have more leisure time and money. There are three key growth areas in hotels: (1) economy hotels, (2) suites (hotels are being built with nothing but suites and the price is equal to that of a good hotel room), and (3) downtown properties. Also hot are the resort business (in and outside of the United States) and gambling. The dynamic jobs include marketing (because everything is so competitive), food and beverage, and casino operations.

Where women are concerned, Korn/Ferry International's *Profile of Women Senior Executives* revealed that the average woman senior executive was most often with "a firm in the commercial banking/diversified financial services sector." It's a fast growing industry that is also undergoing a lot of changes and one that has and will continue to offer opportunities for women in management. Women in financial services tend to be younger than other women executives surveyed. The compensation in the field is slightly less than the national average, although the insurance industry is at the bottom. (It also tends to pay men less.) It is, however, least likely to ask you to relocate.

*The Wall Street Journal* summed up high-tech. "Women managers rise in high-tech, but they are still a rare breed."

Women executives in industrial companies are among the second highest paid, but are also pretty scarce. More make it to top management who have legal backgrounds.

Women retail executives are the highest paid and, as in the banking area, have gained great acceptance. They are *most* likely to be asked to relocate.

## WORK FOR A QUALITY COMPANY AND PREFERABLY IN A MAJOR CITY

Headhunters search for talent in quality companies. Their clients don't want people from questionable firms. They want proven executive ability demonstrated in a high-caliber environment. Quality is generally synonymous with the large firms, but not limited to them. However, most executives are pulled from big companies (or the larger ones in their industry) to other big companies and smaller operations. Rule of thumb: more searches are done for giants. If you work for one you'll get more calls.

Most large companies tend to be headquartered in major cities. Obviously this is where the search action is. If you work for a good company, but in the boondocks, you are out-of-sight and out-of-mind to most headhunters who generally cast their nets in a metropolitan area first. Clients ideally want to avoid the expense of relocating executives. So they have headhunters look locally—in the large city in which they are located and its environs—before widening the loop to neighboring cities. But where very senior level searches are concerned, there are rarely geographic limitations; the best candidate is the target. Of course searches are done for smaller companies, located in smaller towns. Some search firms have even built a specialty doing this.

---

A search firm was asked to find a chief financial officer for the Navaho Indian tribe. The finalist had to be approved by the 72-man council. The position would be in a small Arizona town. After extensive searching, a candidate from Guam was found who thought the location was paradise.

---

For the past several years, according to the *National Index of Executive Vacancies,* the bulk of executive hiring has been in the east and west—accounting for approximately 75 percent of it. The midwest, southeast, and southwest comprise the remainder.

## SELF-PROMOTE, BE VERY VISIBLE—
## TO YOUR MANAGERS, AMONG YOUR PEERS,
## WITH CLIENTS, AND IN GENERAL

If you are well-known and, naturally, good at what you do, you're more likely to be considered for senior posts when they arise. When headhunters call their contacts (who could be any of the aforementioned groups) looking for leads—they are more likely to think of you.

How can you promote yourself? Write articles or a book. Give speeches. Join quality organizations—professional/business, civic/community, or social. And ideally hold office.

Edward Wakin, Ph.D. (professor of communications at Fordham University) in his article "Good Things Come To Those Who Join" (*Today's Office*) says, "Career strategists agree that joining clubs and associations is a must for executives on the rise. Joiners, they say, demonstrate that they have the drive necessary to be successful."

Which organizations are the best to join? The ones that make you most visible, provide the best contacts, keep you most informed, enhance your image, and are most popular with your management.

Community involvement shows your interest in issues beyond yourself and many companies require their management to participate in such organizations. Holding an office gets you more involved with potentially important senior contacts. Additionally,

Korn/Ferry International's study of female senior executives showed that the average executive woman belonged to women's groups and private clubs.

## HAVE A QUALITY EDUCATION

Of lesser importance in getting a headhunter to call, though not to be overlooked, is one's educational background. A good education helps you obtain the best jobs, in the most dynamic fields, and with the finest companies. Its impact is greater at the onset of one's career. Work performance is *ultimately* more important. Most men and women senior executives have undergraduate degrees and many have MBAs or law degrees. Graduate school enrollments have increased over the past several years and naturally the quality schools are the most popular.

The Arthur Young & Company *CEO* study showed that about 41 percent have advanced degrees and that most chief executives rate MBA holders ahead of other employees.

Similarly, the Heidrick and Struggles *Mobile Manager* study found that more than half of the participants held two degrees. Nevertheless, educational credentials were deemed least important in moving up.

In the Korn/Ferry International studies, BA degrees outranked BSs among senior executives. Most male senior executives went to Harvard for their MBA; New York University was second. For women, NYU had the most students, with the University of Chicago and Columbia thereafter. Educational levels versus income yielded an interesting point regarding women—MBAs and PhDs weren't generally the top earners.

The Arthur Young & Company research found, "The Harvard M.B.A. is the single most popular degree." Stanford is second. "At the undergraduate level, it is the Yale bachelor's degree."

The *CEO* profile by Heidrick and Struggles found that, "Harvard maintains its substantial lead among schools from which CEOs have earned degrees."

## BE WILLING TO RELOCATE DOMESTICALLY OR INTERNATIONALLY

Another important though secondary factor in attracting a head-hunter's call is your willingness to relocate domestically or internationally. Obviously if an executive is open to relocating to another city or overseas, a headhunter has additional latitude and can call more often with opportunities. However, as previously mentioned, employers generally recruit locally first in order to avoid costly moving and expatriate expenses—the latter often include free housing; possibly servants; schooling for children; a yearly trip home, and so forth. So the true number of opportunities which exist for the flexible is somewhat reduced. The executive must also consider whether the supposed opportunity is in the town of Podunk, USA or in Oshkosh, Overseas—small, less significant locations where the out-of-sight and out-of-mind syndrome can adversely affect one's growth in a company. Yet some executives who have taken assignments in the Middle East, for example, at inflated wages (and where there are no taxes on the first $75,000 earned) plus many expatriate perks have been able to sock away a modest bankroll. This can enable a better lifestyle on their return to the United States (assuming inflation and high mortgage rates don't erode things). Others feel the loss of company-paid perks when they return.

The Korn/Ferry International executive study revealed the average executive believes in "mobility and that an executive's chances for advancement are greater if he does not remain with one company for his entire career." (Executives in this study were mostly male and had been with their present employer for almost 20 years.) These executives relocated an average of three times during their careers. Only 11 percent transferred overseas, although 64 percent considered overseas exposure valuable to professional growth.

The Korn/Ferry International women's executive profile showed that 33 percent of the respondents had been asked to relocate and 21 percent did (81 percent of the men did). "Of the women who refused to transfer, 21 percent believe refusal hurt their careers."

A transfer is not the same as relocating with a new employer. Nevertheless, the philosophy of senior executives in the studies suggests that the majority of men saw the career advantages of working in more than one geographic location while women did not.

The Heidrick and Struggles *CEO* study showed that about four out of five CEOs have relocated and that nearly half have done so three or more times.

Another Korn/Ferry International study, *The Repatriation of The American International Executive,* demonstrated that "a majority of surveyed executives viewed their international experience as a valuable career advantage. But the assessment appears to represent the long-range perspective." There were many negatives including "loss of advancement vis-à-vis their peers, assignments were not seen as highly advantageous in terms of compensation," nor were they "sure stepping stones to advancement," and so forth. Most, however, said they would consider another, though different, international assignment.

And there are other methods of attracting and holding a headhunter's attention that are discussed in the next chapter.

----------------------------------------------------------— **CHAPTER 6** __

# Getting the Headhunter's Attention— Part Two

## MAKE YOURSELF KNOWN TO A HEADHUNTER BY SENDING HIM A LETTER OR A COVER LETTER AND RESUME

This is the simple, fundamental way to initially make the head-hunter aware of you. If you know someone who knows him, a referral call may not be inappropriate. However, a resume may still be requested. The recruiter, who is busy serving his clients' needs, is typically less desirous of numerous calls of this kind. He'll call you when he has an appropriate situation. Headhunters are not huffy and standoffish about receiving calls, just typically busy taking care of priority number one—doing searches.

Will contacting a headhunter make you appear hungry and almost out of work? It's just a cue to a consultant that you would like to hear about opportunities. You may be unhappy; it doesn't mean more. And now you may occasionally hear from him. Why limit your chances? Many recruiters welcome unsolicited resumes because *every once in a while* one comes in that's a perfect match for an assignment they're doing. It can make their lives easier and they can fill a spot in record time.

What should you do if you're happy at your job, but curious about possible opportunities? The gainfully employed executive should proceed slowly and not flood the market with resumes. Write to a handful of search companies. See what kind of feedback is gotten before sending out another wave of curricula vitae. You may not hear from those you've written to or you may receive an inquiry or two regarding a particular element in your resume. This could lead you to modify your letter or resume, such as expanding on the item that draws attention.

What approach can the soon-to-be-laid-off executive use to expedite sending out his resume? If you're being squeezed out of a position or even if you're unemployed, write to a lot of search companies—it can't hurt. It's unlikely that this will tarnish your image since a company won't get the resume from more than one search firm. As previously mentioned, search firms don't send resumes to clients without first speaking to you about the situation. And since search firms are paid large fees in advance, companies don't retain more than one at a time to work on a specific search. Besides, your need for action outweighs this unlikely concern.

A vice president in the corporate finance group of a Wall Street firm found herself in a tricky situation. Sometime earlier, in continual conflict with an unpleasant boss, and with business falling off, she and management agreed she should leave. She sent out resumes to search firms. Among the various interviews that resulted was one with the relatively small public finance group at a big merchant bank. She met several officers within the bank, including senior management, but ultimately declined an offer. Months later, when she was soon-to-be unemployed, another search firm referred her to the same bank's active private placement group. Line managers in the two groups had the authority to retain whichever search firm they liked—not uncommon in many companies. Furthermore, the bank was so large, neither manager knew that the other had met her—not at all uncommon in large companies. The second manager also liked her and prior to an offer mentioned a meeting with the brass. She then told him and the search firm about her previous visit. Although they would have preferred knowing about this earlier on, they didn't view it unfavorably. The woman was hired and both search firms were paid.

What if an executive makes contact with a headhunter at a large search firm and is then given an opportunity, through a personal acquaintance, to meet another recruiter in that office—is it appropriate to follow up the second meeting? Yes. Big search firms have many partners and each has his own client following. So another contact can be useful although it isn't necessary in many cases because internal dialogues and the research department bridge the gap. However, do tell the parties involved that you have already spoken to an officer in the company, but you would welcome meeting another if it is beneficial.

*The Wall Street Journal* reported, "Atari Corp. told its fired managers they had two days to clear out." If an executive is mailing out 100 resumes ASAP because he is being cut with short notice, he can write to the managing partner or general manager without knowing his name (although writing to a specific person is better). In most large search firms, all quality mail-in resumes circulate to staff or a summary sheet outlining backgrounds serves instead. Or, the research department gets them for future use. This is a quick way to cover ground.

How does an executive know which search firms to write to? Speak to friends and find out which they have dealt with satisfactorily. They may even be able to recommend a specific consultant and that can expedite. The Association of Executive Search Consultants produces a list of its member firms (about 70) which briefly indicates the area they specialize in. Write or call and the brochure will be sent at a very nominal cost. They are located at 151 Railroad Avenue in Greenwich, Connecticut 06830; (203) 661-6606. It's by no means a full representation of the many search firms which exist nor does it have all of the giants. *The Directory of Executive Recruiters,* by Consultants News, James Kennedy, editor, comes closer to the mark. It lists hundreds of search firms, their locations, and the fields and industries in which they specialize. It is available in libraries or can be purchased at a nominal cost by writing or calling: Consultants Bookstore, Templeton Road, Fitzwilliam, New Hampshire 03447; (603) 585-2200, 6544.

In summary, there is no complete short list of top notch large and medium sized firms which would make life easier for the executive. As a starter, pending your need to obtain broader lists such as the aforementioned, several high quality firms, often having multiple offices (many internationally) and general practices for the most part, are listed below. Check your telephone directory for the address nearest you.

Korn/Ferry International

Russell Reynolds Associates, Inc.

Heidrick and Struggles, Inc.

Spencer Stuart & Associates

Ward Howell International, Inc.

Boyden Associates, Inc.

Lamalie Associates, Inc.

Paul R. Ray & Co., Inc.

Handy Associates, Inc.

Nordeman Grimm, Inc.

Egon Zehnder International, Inc.

Witt Associates Inc. (health care only)

Haley Associates, Inc.

Canny, Bowen Inc.

Paul Stafford Associates, Ltd.

Rather than contact the general managers, it is wiser to call and find out which recruiter serves *your* field. Why miss an opportunity to possibly establish a rapport with the right headhunter? If there are several—pick one. In a small office, the general manager may be the right person. He will usually pass "mail-ins" along. If you are interested in working in more than one major city (despite computerization and resume retrieval ability) write to specific headhunters in each location using the aforementioned approach. Many searches are conducted locally, but if a good resume comes in from elsewhere, it might generate interest.

What does a search company do with its resumes? They are cross-coded and filed by one's industry, position, and residence (city and state). With more sophisticated firms, entries are made in their data processing system. Resumes deemed unsuitable (one's wages may not be at the search firm's threshold, the person's field is one they don't work in, the person has job-hopped, or been unemployed for some time) are not kept.

What can the executive expect from a search firm? That his correspondence will be filed or computerized if he meets the company's parameters. The major firms get considerable mail and form letters are often used to acknowledge them. Sometimes an executive doesn't get an initial reply from the headhunter or search firm he wrote to. It may be their rudeness—unless no feedback was necessary. However, many smaller firms usually don't reply to mail-in resumes and many disregard them. They can't afford to acknowledge and file them all. This may change with the advent of minicomputers. The executive will get a call if and when a match exists between his background and a search. He may not hear from the firm for months because there was no current match. A form letter may arrive reflecting your employer is a client of theirs and therefore they can't work with you. Your anonymity will be protected. The "I'm sorry, but we have nothing now" reply may be done with a personalized telephone call. This is often the case if the headhunter wants to source you or, if you are influential, to get on your good side because you may be able to retain him in the future. It's an opportunity for you to pump him with some questions. Sometimes the headhunter will even conduct a "courtesy" interview. One recruiter interviewed an executive vice president who was planning to leave his firm, although he had no job in mind for him. Career counseling was offered and an amiable hour was spent together. They didn't communicate during the next six months. Then the executive telephoned as the financial representative of a billionaire sheik who wanted to retain the headhunter to do a few very high paying searches.

If the executive doesn't hear from a search firm and months go by, even if he's had an earlier acknowledgment, what should he do? He should recorrespond. Resumes sometimes get lost. His pretext may be an addition to his list of responsibilities, a change in assignment, or a new accomplishment. This keeps his name in front of the recruiter in an acceptable way. When a resume is sent to a specific consultant, it sometimes may not get into the master file. The headhunter may have it in his files per a particular search and it never circulated. It is still advisable to write to a specific consultant where you may have an opportunity to develop a personal rapport with someone with contacts, as opposed to writing to a research department, even though this will guarantee your resume in a data bank. Your best bet is to do both.

Some executives do not have a resume, nor do they plan to write one. Their aim is to inform a few select search firms of their interest in occasionally hearing about a situation. They are basically happy at work and will very unaggressively put a toe in the water. They send out a couple of letters describing themselves which are very much like resumes because they are a few pages long and describe, often in detail, their career objectives, strengths, work history, and education—and provide personal data. They occasionally and desirably include location preferences, current compensation, publications, languages, and so forth. The message, however, because it's a letter, is that they are not really looking and are highly selective.

The same can be accomplished with a cover letter and a resume even though having the latter indicates more of a willingness to hear about opportunities. You've gone to the expense and trouble to print up an autobiography. Yet the cover letter can temper this and specify very particular objectives. It is usually brief—a few sentences or short paragraphs—and describes career objectives and strengths, while succinctly summarizing one's work history and education. Mentioning location preferences and one's compensation is useful.

Many executives, whether they submit letters or cover letters and resumes, open their correspondence with the notion that they are not merely looking for a job. Rather they indicate an awareness that search firms often work on unusual assignments that may not be publicized in other ways. They want to hear about these plums—nothing more! It's a good strategy.

Should you mention your compensation? There are different schools of thought on this issue. Search firms like it because headhunters can quickly determine if you are priced right for an assignment which they are working on. That is, you're not earning much too little or much too much, and this saves a telephone call, a possible interview, and lost time on both sides. Executives feel it delimits their presentation and crimps the ability to negotiate for bigger dollars. The fact is that headhunters will pretty quickly ask about your income in order to determine your suitability, in part, for a situation. Most will not refer you to a client without first gaining this information. There is no bluffing here as references, including compensation, will be checked. So take your pick whether to be initially open or not.

And, by the way, no photographs please. They are irrelevant to the point where the former research director of a major search firm kept a mug shot bulletin board of all the uglies she received. No VCR resume tapes either. There may be a firm or two who work in this manner, but most either lack the hardware for viewing or can't afford the time. Don't use sexy colored paper either—let your personal stationery or standard bond plus your track record speak for itself. And you can only put a recruiter off by the kind of juvenile high jinks shown by the marketing executive who included with his cover letter and resume a wallet size photo of himself in bermuda shorts and a sport shirt with his arm around a scantily clad woman. Or, the wise guy, John Smith, who sent a picture of himself standing next to a huge statue of Buddha. Captioned in parenthesis, "John Smith on right."

The following are full letter and cover letter samples.

## FULL LETTER I

Thomas H. Jones
18 Clearview Road
Scarsdale, New York 11208

January 12, 1986

Mr. Joseph Search
Headhunters, Inc.
One Park Avenue
New York, NY 10001

Dear Mr. Search:

Since it behooves a savvy, ambitious executive to make himself known to a high quality executive search firm, such as yours—an ideal assignment for me may come your way—the following will tell you more about a very successful, gainfully employed (yet always willing to selectively listen to an opportunity) senior banker.

My aim is to ultimately run a large quality bank while near term becoming the director of corporate lending for such an institution whether it be domestic, foreign, or perhaps a major regional one—regardless of location.

My strong suits include 20 years of diverse lending experience gained at two major banks and on four continents. There are few products and services with which I lack familiarity. And I have managed over 200 people, recruited and developed teams, and greatly expanded portfolios and profitability.

Currently, I am the executive vice president and director of marketing for the Total Bank of Switzerland, where I have been employed for 15 years. As the number two man in this country, reporting to the bank's president, my duties include the management of five lending groups in New York: American, International, Commodities, Swiss, and Correspondent. The total staff is 45 and the combined portfolios approach $2 billion. Additionally, a marketing and product development group of 10 reports to me. The bank has seven branches in other major U.S. cities, with a combined staff of 145 and portfolios equaling $3 billion, which are also my responsibility. I joined the bank as a vice president/manager of corporate banking and was promoted to senior vice president in 1977 and to executive vice president in 1982. We only had a New York branch, a staff of 35 and a $1 billion portfolio when I arrived. Over the ensuing years, the president and I built the operation to its present level—the most profitable entity in the entire Total Bank system worldwide.

I would add that the diverse and major client relationships which we enjoy were primarily pioneered by myself through numerous trips around the country and the world, calling on prospects, converting them to accounts and then expanding the dealings.

The bank takes good care of me and I am quite happy. My salary approaches $175,000 and bonuses have ranged to $50,000, plus a car, clubs, and a low mortgage rate. However, the institution has recently suffered losses in other parts of the world through poor investments and a trading casualty. The impact will curtail U.S. expansion for several years. At 46 years of age, I ideally do not want to merely mind the store for the next five years. On the other hand, management has informed me that I will be the next president—an unusual opportunity for an American.

Prior to being recruited to Total, I was vice president and team leader in the multinational lending group at Citibank where I managed a $1.5 billion portfolio and a staff of five. I worked there for five years, becoming a vice president in record time, and also completing their management training program.

I previously obtained a MBA from Harvard's Graduate School of Business; spent over three years in the U.S. Army (Vietnam) discharging as a captain and Silver Star recipient, and received a BA in English at Columbia University.

I am married, with three children and my outside interests include tennis, golf, and travel.

I look forward to occasionally hearing from you, and if

you think it beneficial, perhaps we can meet over lunch or a drink. Naturally, if I can be of any assistance to you with your assignments, please call: (O) 212 555-2682, (H) 914 555-1986.

Sincerely,

Thomas H. Jones

Full letters, unlike resumes, enable self-expression and personality to shine through although they take longer to skim. The reverse chronological order with which Jones laid out his background is desirable. Compensation, though not specific, suggests the upper end—a middle ground if you don't like full or prefer no disclosure. Aside from his being influential, what wise headhunter could resist at least calling and acknowledging the letter since the no doubt well-connected gentleman could aid as a source with financial searches or possibly retain his services.

## COVER LETTER I

18 Clearview Road
Scarsdale, New York 11208
January 12, 1986

Mr. Joseph Search
Headhunters, Inc.
One Park Avenue
New York, NY 10001

Dear Mr. Search:
It pays to let a quality search firm know of you—even if you're happy—just in case something special comes across their desk.

Accordingly, I am interested in hearing about senior level lending/management positions which could lead to running a domestic or foreign bank. I'm open to relocation.

I am the executive vice president/director of marketing and number two man in a major international bank where I have been employed for 15 years. My responsibilities include worldwide corporate lending, management of 200 people and eight offices throughout the United States, and combined portfolios totaling $5 billion. Successes include building the staff from 35, the offices from one, and the portfolio from $1 billion. The operation has become the bank's most profitable one worldwide and I will be its next president.

I began my career at Citibank, after receiving an MBA from Harvard.

My total compensation approaches $225,000 plus attractive perks.

I welcome hearing from you and, if you think it's beneficial, perhaps we can meet over a drink or lunch. If I can be a source with a tough search, please call (O) 212 555-2682, (H) 914 555-1986.

Sincerely,


Thomas H. Jones


The resume (accompanying the cover letter) provides all details including the undergraduate degree. With a top MBA it isn't necessary to mention the BA in a cover letter. And you needn't state in the letter that the enclosed resume provides details because it's obvious. Likewise, the Citicorp and army experiences aren't respectively developed or mentioned because they're not initially relevant. The "grabber" or successes in Jones's career tell enough to make a headhunter turn the page.

Avoid the following type of cover letter; it's too bossy, negative, and paranoid.

## COVER LETTER 2

Dear Mr. Search:
   I believe it is important for us to meet and talk. Please give me a call at my office (leave only your name) so we can set up an appointment. My present employer doesn't know that I'm looking for a new job (and I don't want them to know); be discreet. My resume is enclosed.

Resumes can have several formats; there is no best one! When search firms write them, they are usually two or three pages in length. The former is recommended and a one page version is also fine. Headhunters and prospective employers want to get at the facts quickly. It should begin with one's name, address, and telephone numbers, and continue, including dates, with your educational background, business history, and military experience. The current position is listed first. Omit career goals—why limit yourself—this gets mentioned in the cover letter. Responsibilities are explained and all promotions and achievements are highlighted. Current ones first and then work backwards. The resume may include a special accomplishments section mentioning publications (another separate area if large), awards, and select memberships. Close with a personal data section—if you are inclined—the law prohibits such inquiry by prospective employers. However, it is desirable information. Include age, marital, and family status. If you still have room, mention some outside interests. Don't state that references are available on request—it's understood. Avoid long-winded descriptions and the excessive use of adjectives. Use concise statements without extensive explanations. You can talk through the details when you're with the headhunter. Use verbs to begin most sentences because these action words make you appear to be a doer. And if your resume is professionally prepared by a service, make sure it sounds like you wrote it.
   Avoid the extraneous. In the personal information section, one fellow included the color of his hair and eyes, and the fact that he was left-handed. He also noted that his parents were de-

ceased. Another chap, in the interests area, mentioned travel, leisurely weekend morning bicycle rides, and going out to breakfast.

In the business history portion of his resume, some joker who was employed by a commode company described his work in terms of his "full bottom line responsibility."

The following are two examples of resumes.

## RESUME I

### THOMAS H. JONES

| | |
|---|---|
| 18 Clearview Road | (H) 914 555-1986 |
| Scarsdale, New York 11208 | (O) 212 555-2682 |

#### EDUCATION

| | |
|---|---|
| Harvard Graduate School of Business | Columbia University |
| MBA—Finance—1967 | BA—English—1962 |

#### BUSINESS HISTORY

*Total Bank of Switzerland;* New York, NY (1972–Present)
Executive vice president and director of marketing

Number two man in the United States and report to the president. Manage 200 people in five New York-based groups (American, International, Commodities, Swiss, and Correspondent), seven branches (Atlanta, Miami, Chicago, Houston, Denver, San Francisco, and Los Angeles) and a marketing/product development group. Combined portfolios total $5 billion. Developed the bank from a New York branch of 35 people and a $1 billion portfolio. Pioneered and grew numerous diverse lending relationships on four continents. The U.S. operation has become the most profitable entity in the organization worldwide. Promoted to executive vice president in 1982 and senior vice president in 1977. Joined as vice president/manager—corporate banking.

*Citibank;* New York, NY (1967–1972)
Vice president/team leader

Managed staff of five and $1.5 billion portfolio of multinational Fortune 1000 clients headquartered in the metropolitan area. Grew the team from three and the portfolio from $1 billion. Progressed through the ranks in record time. Completed management training program.

MILITARY

*U.S. Army;* Vietnam (1962–1965)
Captain

Managed a company with over 200 men; Silver Star recipient.

PERSONAL DATA

Age 46; Married, 3 children
Outside interests include tennis, golf, and travel.

## RESUME 2

### THOMAS H. JONES

18 Clearview Road
Scarsdale, New York 11208
(H) 914 555-1986
(O) 212 555-2682

EDUCATIONAL BACKGROUND

Harvard Graduate School of Business
Boston, MA
MBA—Finance—1967

Columbia University
New York, NY
BA—English—1962

BUSINESS HISTORY

Executive vice president and director of marketing
Total Bank of Switzerland
New York, NY

*1972 to Present*
- ☐ Number two man in the United States and report to the president
- ☐ Manage 200 people in five New York based groups (American, International, Commodities, Swiss, and Correspondent), seven branches (Atlanta, Miami, Chicago, Houston, Denver, San Francisco, and Los Angeles) and a marketing/product development group
- ☐ Manage combined portfolios totaling $5 billion
- ☐ Developed the bank from a New York branch with 35 people and a $1 billion portfolio
- ☐ Pioneered and grew numerous diverse lending relationships on four continents
- ☐ Developed the U.S. operation to the point where it is the most profitable entity in the organization worldwide
- ☐ Promoted to executive vice president in 1982; senior vice president in 1977 and joined as vice president and manager of corporate lending

Vice president and team leader
Citibank
New York, NY

*1967 to 1972*
- ☐ Managed a staff of five and a $1.5 billion portfolio of Fortune 1000 clients headquartered in the metropolitan area
- ☐ Grew the team from three and the portfolio from $1 billion
- ☐ Progressed through the ranks in record time
- ☐ Completed management training program

MILITARY BACKGROUND

Captain
U.S. Army
Vietnam

*1962 to 1965*
☐ Managed a company with over 200 men
☐ Silver Star recipient

PERSONAL DATA
☐ Born 7-9-40; married, three children
☐ Outside interests include tennis, golf, and travel

## MAKE YOURSELF LIKED BY A HEADHUNTER

We've touched on it, but another important way to attract a recruiter's attention is to *make yourself liked by a headhunter by being a source regarding candidates and market information (which company has a search need, which just lost an executive, whom to contact, what trends you've seen . . . ).*

These are a headhunter's "hot buttons." This is how he makes a living—finding new search needs, filling positions and being aware. If you help him, confidentially if preferred, he'll remember you favorably . . . and pay his dues by informing you of appropriate searches when they arise.

So after submitting a resume, you may find it easier to get through to a recruiter and to sustain his attention with marketplace intelligence. Consultants would never get their work done if they merely chatted all day. Don't call every three months and say "Hi." But if you have something relevant to say, it will keep your name current in the headhunter's mind.

# CHAPTER 7

# What To Do
# When a Headhunter Calls

"Good morning. This is Joe Search of Headhunters, Inc. We're doing a search for a major New England bank which is looking for a president and chief operating officer. I wondered if you would be interested in hearing some details about it?"

So begins the headhunter's typical telephone approach.

## HOW SHOULD YOU HANDLE IT?

Responses run the gamut. From:

---

"Sounds interesting. Tell me more about it."

"Hmm. Let me close my door . . . "

"I'm in the middle of a meeting/rushing off to one/late for an appointment. Can I call you back?/Can you call me back in an hour?/Can you call me at home?" (This is infrequently requested.)

"I'm not interested, but I know someone who is."

---

To:

---

"How did you get my name?"

"I'm sorry, but I don't know your firm."

"Haven't heard from one of you guys in the last few weeks. Am I losing my touch or has the market gone soft?"

"I'm not interested, but my wife/son/daughter/nephew or niece might be." (This only happened once.)

"I don't need an Auntie Mame to put me together with a company."

"Not interested," and immediately hangs up. (Thankfully this happens very rarely.)

---

If the headhunter's call hasn't caught you off guard or at a busy moment and you feel sufficiently composed and interested, explore the situation. But if you're busy or a colleague is too close to enable a private dialogue, then simply say so and arrange for another time to converse. It doesn't matter who calls whom back, although it is good manners to suggest returning the call. You do not appear hungry by doing so.

Needless to say, don't be unnecessarily rude to a fellow businessman—you or a friend may need him in the future. Even presidents get impeached. When a really special job develops in your field, the consultant won't call you again. In fact, you may have hung up on it!

And of course, be a source if you're not interested. It's good for everyone concerned.

Sometimes people are overly concerned about how their name was obtained. In many instances, headhunters were given the lead by a mutual acquaintance and can identify this source. Names are also obtained from directories or a headhunter's being aware of your achievements because he tracks your field. Occasionally, consultants can't divulge their source because your name was given confidentially. Who would do that and why? It's generally a friend of the recruiter's, in your field, who doesn't know you personally, but respects your work and is helping out the headhunter. It may be someone who knows you, though not personally, and respects you but doesn't know if you are in the market. Search is obviously a people network business and you shouldn't be surprised when your name is given out in this manner. It's flattering. The parties offering your name are also motivated by a desire to endear themselves to the recruiter. Some are just fair-minded businessmen simply doing a favor!

Aside from the assistant director of a department who recommends his boss, in confidence, to clear the way for his succession (rare), another (very rare) experience comes to mind . . .

A well regarded executive who had grown unhappy with his situation sent several resumes to different search firms. No employment leads were generated so he sent out more resumes. One or two replies developed. He then had an unrelated altercation with his manager, an irritable type who was the key reason for his desire to move on. During the next few days, he received calls from several headhunters—some of whom he hadn't written to! He lunched with one of the latter and although they had a nice rapport, couldn't find out exactly how he came to telephone him. Nothing more developed, but the two men stayed in touch. Months later, the executive accepted a position via another search firm's introduction. A year later and over a lunch which he called with the former recruiter, he unearthed that his exmanager had asked the fellow, "Get that thorn out of my side."

Two other executives who reported to the ogre were reputed to be composing a resume on him; they knew about his previous experience and were planning to multiply submit it to various headhunters. Management miraculously though unsuspectingly came to their aid and transferred the man to the employee relations department as its new chief.

If you receive a call from a firm unknown to you, you may want to check them out with the Association of Executive Search Consultants' list or the *Directory of Executive Recruiters* first. Then call them back.

## CONTINUING THE TELEPHONE CONVERSATION

If you decide to continue the telephone conversation with the headhunter, whether it be on the first call or a subsequent one, what typically happens and what do you do next?

Basically, you're going to indicate a mild interest or curiosity by asking him to explain more about the assignment or his client. He will briefly do that. It's okay to ask questions. If you are still intrigued, tell him. Otherwise, he will ask if you are, in order to move the situation along. The recruiter will then ask you a few questions to determine your suitability for the position. If he decides you are a possible fit, he'll suggest getting together.

The headhunter will generally not tell you the name of his client at this stage. You can ask, but he'll probably only tell you the industry they're in, approximate location and size, and give you a feel for their general activities. It will be enough for you to go on, initially. That's the mutual anonymity ingredient in a search— for clients and candidates. He will also give you an overview of the position's key responsibilities: title, whom it reports to, basic duties, number of people managed, location, and perhaps the promotional potential. He may indicate compensation. If he doesn't, feel free to inquire as it can obviously be a quick spur or detriment to your interest. You can ask any questions that are pertinent to you, but ideally keep them relevant to this first level dialogue. Don't get into benefits questions about the amount of vacation time or minutia as to whether there is a dental plan. If the company, job, and money seem right, meet the headhunter to explore details.

## QUESTIONS HEADHUNTERS ASK

Questions headhunters typically ask over the telephone include: title, key responsibilities, successes, length of time with present company, and compensation. You can "ball park" the latter if you prefer. He may go back a position or two and briefly cover some of this ground.

The conversation may run 5, 10, or more minutes. It can also take 60 seconds. If the recruiter knows of you as a real factor in a field in which he is now searching, he may not even screen you. He'll bait his hook and describe the assignment. If you nibble, he'll suggest meeting. This can also happen when the client gives the headhunter a short list of 10 to 20 people whom they would like. You're one and you bite.

There is no great mystery to the talk between the two parties: the headhunter and you. Keep your rational, business hat on. It's the stuffy or inflated presentation of your credentials and self-worth that dissuades a recruiter. It's often the most senior executives who are the most gentlemanly, straightforward and unpretentious.

Some recruiters develop an abridged resume during the initial telephone chat, as opposed to a few notes. Their clients may want to see the backgrounds of potential candidates in writing before they green light personal interviews. The headhunter may therefore tell you who the client is since your name may be presented. He may also mail you a position description and an annual report. This method is used extensively with out-of-town executives. If the recruiter is based in New York and develops candidates in Chicago, Los Angeles, or Houston, he'll also spend more time on the telephone exploring backgrounds prior to arranging personal interviews.

If the headhunter isn't sure you're right for his situation or if you live far away, he may ask you to send him a resume in order to better evaluate you. It's a reasonable request, if you have one, because it saves time on the telephone. Assuming you don't, tell him and suggest (what he'd probably do anyway) that you're willing to spend additional time on the telephone with him outlining your background. If he insists on a resume, he's probably not too interested in you. Your appetite for the job in question should determine your willingness to comply.

## SETTING UP A MEETING

When the telephone conversation between the headhunter and the executive ultimately yields mutual interest—the position described is of some interest to you and he thinks you may be qualified—the headhunter will suggest meeting. This is typically done during business hours, but can be before 9 A.M. and after 5 P.M. If the parties are near each other or within a commute of a few hours, the get-together is generally in the recruiter's office or at a restaurant or club near him. Busy and satisfied senior executives may lobby for the recruiter coming to them and get their way. A mutually convenient appointment is arranged. Usually the consultant tries to draw the recruiter to his office—it's more convenient and private. Dining meetings can run two hours and if either party quickly decides that the situation isn't right precious time is wasted, although it is a pleasant and relaxed way to do business. Drinks are an alternative, particularly for those who don't wish to be seen in a search firm's office. However, they have as much security in an office as they do in a public place. It's hard for a headhunter to take good notes at the dinner table or at a bar; it's also conspicuous. He may have to spend additional time completing the information gathering over the telephone. And there's a rehashing element involved. So take your pick.

If the candidate lives out of town, several hours or a plane ride away, or overseas, the headhunter may ask if he plans to visit his city in the very near future. When this is the case, an appointment is easily arranged. Should the executive have no such plans, the recruiter will suggest either flying him in and paying his way so they can meet or going to his hometown. Headhunters generally prefer to fly you in because the time spent traveling is less productive than being in their offices. Unless they have other candidates or business calls in your city, expect to be invited to visit them. And they'll cover all expenses for taxis, plane, hotel and meals, even mileage and parking if you drive your own car. They'll suggest you book the most convenient flight, using your credit card, and they'll reimburse you. Most search firms will recommend traveling business class unless you are a very senior executive. Get receipts where you can for your expenditures.

Once again, busy executives may not have the time or desire to travel to the recruiter and they say so. Then it's the consultants' problem to get to you, if they're really interested. Do what is best for you. Mutually difficult travel schedules have cost a possible candidate a position. In this regard, meetings have been set up in airports so the busy executive and headhunter can do something akin to "two ships passing in the night."

A Philadelphia based brokerage house manager was interested in the position which the New York based recruiter described over the telephone. The recruiter had no plans to be in Philadelphia, but the executive was coming to New York with his wife that weekend for dinner and a show. "Can you find an extra hour so that we can meet?" asked the headhunter. "I'm on a very tight schedule so I'm afraid not. Unless . . . care to join my wife and me over dinner?" It was unorthodox, but very acceptable. The headhunter picked up the tab. And the executive later got the job.

CHAPTER 8

# Handling the First Meeting with a Headhunter

The female associate to a senior partner in a major search firm was asked to call a high-powered, young, advertising talent and invite him to breakfast in order to discuss a position. Making the arrangements, she indicated that, "Mr. Jones from my office will . . . ." "You needn't go into your personal life," interjected the prospective candidate. "You don't understand. . . . " She tried to explain, but he cut her off again. "I'll meet you both, no problem." The next morning, the consultants were joined by a slick adman and a woman who showed that her interest was in him and not in the professional purpose of the breakfast meeting. He got the girl, not the job.

## ATTIRE

The way you dress, the way you act, even the way you greet a headhunter on a first meeting are as important as any job interview.

---

"I'm going to be on vacation when I meet you," said the candidate, "so I'll be dressed informally—I won't be wearing a suit." "I'm not going to be on vacation," replied the headhunter, "and neither is my client."

---

On the other hand, a successful stockbroker in his early thirties visited a search firm in a torn sweater, wrinkled denim slacks, and moccasins. "I'm taking the day off," he said. "After I finish talking to you, I'm going sailing." This independent soul was testing the headhunter and through him, a prospective employer—broadcasting his unwillingness to white-collar it and play the game, sufficiently satisfied with his job and ambivalent about looking for a new one. He was not introduced to the recruiter's client for the obvious reasons, although because of his business success, he *could* have been considered—very selectively—for a different client.

Despite the absence of a suit or even a sports jacket, a computer specialist wearing a shirt, a thin black leather tie and casual slacks was referred to a client. The man was gifted in data processing and management information systems and held a PhD in the field from a top school. He also had a fine technical record with his present employer. The headhunter's client badly needed, and was having difficulty recruiting, someone with this man's skills. And the referral was made although the candidate was unwilling to comply with the consultant's suggestion that he wear a suit to his first meeting with the client, a meeting with two group vice presidents. "I'll take it under advisement," he said. Both the headhunter and the client, as it turned out, were willing to take a gamble—in this newer field—on an executive with a nonconformist style.

The vice president, director of marketing for a billion dollar company, headquartered in a suburban city, flew into New York to meet with a headhunter whose client was pin-striped and buttoned-down. Tall, handsome, athletic-looking, affable, articulate—he had style—but he wore a just barely acceptable tan cotton-polyester suit, unacceptable argyle socks, and rust colored, sporty loafers.

A candidate showed up for his first meeting with a recruiter in Levis and a sweater. Sensing the recruiter's disapproval, he said, "I'm going to the garage after we talk." He was the general manager of a bus corporation. "The garage has 140 buses. Twenty are probably half apart and in thick grease on the floor. I'm dressed for what I do. Besides, I couldn't maintain a rapport with my men if I dressed in a pin-stripe." The man made his point. He was also bright, and he was referred. He came in second.

Atypical examples, but they highlight a key point about attire. Unless you are a genius, a great creative artist, or aware that the headhunter or his client are flamboyant (this is rarely the case!), wear conservative business clothes—preferably a dark suit, a white shirt and conventional tie, dark knee-length socks and dark well-shined shoes. Women should wear a version of this too—perhaps substituting a blouse and necklace for the shirt and tie. Otherwise, your chances of being referred may be hurt. Most often you won't be referred at all. Lack of color-coordinated furnishings, and cheap or worn garments can prejudice a first meeting. A recruiter may make a suggestion regarding one's dress, if he thinks it will be accepted without offending. He's likely to do it, however, only when he believes the executive's credentials are otherwise satisfactory.

Interviews are a two-way street. An executive may want to be himself and work where he is accepted for who he is. It may also take this person longer to connect. Depending on the field, however, he may *have* to change his style.

You are measured by the search consultant from the onset—for technical abilities in relation to a job description as well as for personal fit or potential chemistry with the client. A candidate's overall presentation is also weighed and examined in relation to other candidates. So it pays to look neat and be cordial.

If possible, visit the rest room and freshen up before meeting the recruiter. One executive, in a handsome custom-tailored suit did so, but forgot to zip his fly!

The winter wind gave another candidate's longish hair such an eccentric blowing that it was hard to keep from chuckling in spite of his being a highly serious and successful vice president.

## CANCELLATIONS AND STANDUPS

Ideally, don't cancel more than one appointment with the recruiter.

The senior vice president of a modest-sized manufacturing firm sent a resume and a well-written letter to a search partner indicating he would call for an appointment. The consultant didn't have a match, but the letter was catchy, he had spare time, and an appointment was set up. On the appointed day, the senior vice president's secretary called to cancel and reschedule. When that day came around, the secretary called to do the same. The consultant politely said that his calendar was frightfully busy for the next several weeks, or was it years, and that regretfully he couldn't see him. If the officer had personally telephoned, even subsequent to the cancellation via his secretary, things might have been righted.

Don't stand an executive recruiter up. They bleed and lose time like everyone else. Why antagonize unnecessarily?

A headhunter arranged to meet a candidate at O'Hare Airport

in Chicago. He flew there, on time from New York, but the man wasn't there. After waiting nearly a half hour, he telephoned him. "I was there," claimed the executive, "but I'm too tied up to return."

## SALUTATIONS

Salutations can be perfectly commonplace, or they may, in fact, set up unfortunate repercussions in the headhunter's mind.

A former All-American wrestler, now a partner in a renowned investment banking firm, all but crushed the bones in a searcher's hand upon greeting him. Was he merely overenthusiastic or hostile-dominant-aggressive?

A headhunter escorted an executive vice president of a major company into his office and invited him to be seated. The candidate unhesitatingly walked to the consultant's desk and seated himself behind it. Looking up, he surveyed the room . . . then his eyes lit on the aghast recruiter . . . who helplessly stood, mouth open, as if his toy had been confiscated. Blushing with the sudden recognition of what he had unconsciously done, the executive rose and took another chair. The consultant scurried to his throne.

---

"Good morning and how are you?" said Ms. Search to the executive as she ushered him from the reception room toward her office. "O.K.," he said, "but you know what it's like. You must be my age." "No, I'm not!" she replied indignantly.

---

"Due to the high level of this search," said the recruiter to the executive, "I invited a senior colleague to join us." But before he could introduce the president of his company, the candidate said, "It's the kind of professionalism I'd expect of this firm. Why when yachting with your president last summer . . . ." "Excuse me," interjected the president, who had never met him before. "I don't want to embarrass you, but I'm the president." A moment of deadly silence followed. Then the executive said, "Jesus, how you've changed."

Obviously, avoid any of the aforementioned.

## AND DESPITE THE BEST PREPARATIONS . . .

Despite the best preparation by the headhunter and candidate, the unexpected can occur.

A recruiter arrived late for an airport meeting. As he scurried to the rendezvous, he heard himself being paged. Upon arriving at the prearranged location, he discovered a Frenchman with the same surname as his protesting to an executive. "But monsieur, I am not expecting to meet anyone." "Come on man," the candidate answered incredulously. "Let's get it together here."

A headhunter, whom we'll call Harrison, described himself to a candidate and arranged to meet him in front of the Hilton Hotel bar. Arriving early, the headhunter went to a nearby telephone to call his office. The call took longer than he expected, and when he returned to the bar area, 10 minutes late, the candidate was not there. About five minutes later, a man with the right appearance approached him and asked, "Are you Mr. Harrison from Headhunters, Inc?"

"Yes," he said.

"Well, you won't believe what just happened. I walked up to a guy who met the description you gave me and asked if he was Mr. Harrison. He said yes; we shook hands and went to the bar. I gave him my resume and he began to read it. When he realized I was in the engineering field, he looked up, confused. Then we figured it all out. He was a headhunter whose name was Harrison, and he was here waiting to meet a candidate of his own."

## ETIQUETTE, STYLE, PRESENCE, AND POISE

Regarding these four attributes, which wise men bear, please consider the following.

A division president, earning over $250,000 a year in a good-sized company, put his can of Coke and glass on the table adjacent to his chair, but alas, on top of the consultant's promotional literature. He could easily have moved them over. Instead he left wet rings, ruining the material. It left an impression— a negative one.

It was a tough technical search; the consultant couldn't identify many candidates. The few whom he did were rejected, after interviews, for various reasons. Finally, he developed an individual deep in Connecticut and drove an hour and a half to meet him. As he waited in front of Howard Johnson's, a fat man with an enormous beard and tatty clothes approached. To the recruiter's dismay, the man identified himself as the candidate. Certainly, the client wouldn't consider this character, but out of courtesy, the recruiter had to go through the motions of an interview. So they went inside and over coffee the man began to talk about his work. He was so clear, interesting, and knowledgeable that the headhunter was spellbound. The man was one of those people whose work was his whole life and being. He was totally absorbed in it, and he conveyed this and in turn absorbed his audience.

The headhunter now felt he had the best man for the job. When he relayed information about the candidate's background and appearance to the client, he was told, "I'm not going to have any hairy monster in my plant." The recruiter pleaded with the client to meet the fellow and eventually got him to agree. Several days later, the client called and said, "I just hired your referral."

Postscript. While touring one of the company's plants, this executive was about to be excluded from a demonstration because there were noxious chemicals in the air and a gas mask wouldn't fit over his beard. He shaved it off on the spot!

---

Having flown into the head auditor candidate's city, the search consultant asked him if he knew a quiet spot where they could talk. The gentleman took him to a handsome new club, where he was not a member, and used blarney and charm to get past the receptionist. The client *wanted* a nonstereotypical, extroverted auditor. This man passed the test before the interview began.

---

Over a 10-year period, and while residing with his family in the Middle East, a financial executive made millions of dollars. In his late forties, he returned to Connecticut, bought a working farm, and spent the next few years developing it, getting his house in order and his several kids into schools

and colleges. At age 50, he wanted a job. His manner, however, lacked confidence. "But I'm naive regarding the U.S.
marketplace," he apologized. The consultant who was offering him advice said, "You're self-made. Let the world
know. You have lived every man's dream. You succeeded
early enough to try retirement. Then you rethought your
interests and realized you're too active and energetic to stay
at home. Don't be humble. Brag about your achievements
and abilities."

---

---

The executive was very qualified and the consultant said
he'd like to refer him. The pleased candidate then invited
the recruiter and his wife to a party. Upon arriving, they
found fluorescent multicolored spangles leading from the
street to the doorway of a loft. Inside, toga-clad men and
women who looked like models were drinking enthusiasti-
cally and passing around marijuana joints. The executive
came up to the consultant, placed a gentle hand on his arm
and began to stroke it suggestively. "I'm so glad you could
make it," he said softly. The startled headhunter and his
wife began inching toward the door. The host (and suddenly excandidate) said: "I thought we understood each
other." "I thought we did too," said the headhunter, real-
izing the man would be too avant-garde for his conservative
client!

---

Several minutes into their meeting, the Jewish headhunter told
the executive that he had a Japanese client with a need in his
field. "Oh no," the candidate said. "Those little slanty-eyed Japs
are worse than Yids," thereby grossly insulting both parties and
revealing his unsuitability for the recruiter's list—or at least for his
candidate list.

On a balmy spring day, a well-dressed engineering executive
entered a recruiter's office and proceeded to remove his jacket,

loosen his tie and undo his collar. Then he took a foot of chain from his attache case and while fiddling with it said, "OK, let's begin." But the interview was already over.

Going a step further, perhaps, there was a present day Captain Queeg who took some dozen quarters from his jacket pocket and nervously played them hand to hand. Their interview was also a brief one.

Unlike some of these glaring examples, many of us are not fully aware of what we are doing, how we are presenting ourselves or the nervous mannerisms we display during an interview. Most common are cigarette, paper clip, pen or even rubber band fidgeters. The headhunter, however, *will* notice.

Smoke if you do, but not too much lest one be seen as nervous, tense, and lacking confidence. It is not inappropriate to ask the interviewer if he would mind, particularly where a cigar or pipe is concerned.

A sales manager's rubber band once snapped into the center of the room during his conversation with a consultant. He looked sheepish for a moment, but didn't retrieve it and went on talking as if nothing had happened. Something had.

So you think that some gifted and talented people are overlooked because of inconsequential idiosyncracies? Agreed. But clients impose certain "must-haves" and "must-not-haves" on headhunters—who are their representatives. That's the way it is! Search consultants try to establish flexibility where they can. They also try to screen out potential problems when red-flags are observed.

There are executives who are too loud, who talk over others, who cut off conversations. Some may run successful companies, but they may not always be referred to clients, or invited to cocktail parties.

If the candidate wants "one" cocktail and wine with dinner, why not. But don't overdo it. Have less at luncheons.

A vice president in a large firm took a headhunter to lunch at his club. It was observed that the man's facial muscles twitched slightly and that his fingers had a minor tremor. After two double martinis, prior to the luncheon, he became as calm as can be, without any sign of intoxication.

Suspiciously ruddy complected, the operations manager of a major outfit needed two trembling hands to bring coffee cup to mouth during a breakfast meeting.

Executives have been known to lose a job opportunity at a classy restaurant. Regardless of what you do at home, don't cut up your linguine and eat it with a soup spoon—as did the senior vice president and general manager of a quality overseas bank. One senior executive ordered pancakes with peanut butter and syrup and straightforwardly said, "I like it this way." And don't splash your pasta sauce on the headhunter's tie and shirt—particularly when he's buying! Order simple dishes that are easy to eat.

---

The executive vice president and number three man in a major company explained to the headhunter, while they dined at an expensive French restaurant, that he very much wanted to be the president or chairman of a firm. When the meal was over, he blew his nose in the napkin, left his fork and knife askew and left no doubt in the consultant's mind that he was lucky to be at his present level.

---

## DESCRIBING THE JOB/IDENTIFYING THE COMPANY

Preliminaries completed, and before the actual in-depth interview, the executive recruiter will describe the job and identify the company for whom he is doing the search. He will also go into considerable detail delineating responsibilities, reporting relationships (and the backgrounds and styles of these people), size and scope of the operation, compensation, advancement opportunities, and so forth. Throughout, headhunters are amenable to questions from the candidate. Ask as much as you want about the company and the job offered. It helps headhunters judge you. Some candidates take out pad and pen and interview the headhunter or take notes as they go along. Best not to. Save your note taking for after you've left. It can make you look too detail conscious and detract from your eye contact and presentation. Of course, a note taken here or there is cricket. Consultants will usually provide a written description of the post, an annual report, and other literature about the company. Sometimes the descriptive material isn't offered until after the headhunter has interviewed the executive and determined his qualifications as satisfactory.

When the potential candidate is not interested in the situation presented, he saves everybody time by saying so. He may then be asked if he knows anyone, a confidential referral, who would be qualified and perhaps interested. Chances are, helping the headhunter will help him to remember you in his will—future searches which you might like to hear about.

Shortly after their meeting began, a senior vice president at a major bank said, "I'm really not interested in the spot described, but I wanted to get in front of you so you could see who I am. A resume doesn't tell the whole story. There may be other situations and in meeting me and hearing about my background, you'll be in a better position to match me up with something." The headhunter isn't there to serve the (nervy) interviewee, but rather is paid in advance by a client to fill a specific job. Intrusions on his time will reflect negatively.

Sometimes the executive isn't sure if he wants to pursue an assignment. The meeting ends, without a formal interview, while he goes away to think about or check out the deal. When he calls back the recruiter, assuming interest on the latter's behalf, they usually meet again or the interview is done over the telephone. On other occasions, even though the individual isn't certain of his level of interest, the interview may proceed, for convenience's sake or future reference.

A candidate may inquire about other jobs which the consultant is working on that could be suitable for him—even though he is interested in the position initially described. You are sent to only one client at a time, to avoid conflicts of interest for the recruiter. Naturally, if it doesn't work out and there are other positions available the headhunter will consider you for them.

Infrequently, a recruiter may try to screen or briefly interview someone without having provided a client's name or details of the assignment. It can save time for both parties if he quickly qualifies or disqualifies an executive. No harm, unless he begins to probe and seeks more personal information, such as the customers' names or the names of people the executive reports to. Such divulgence first requires "payment"—the headhunter should tell who his client is and more about the job in question. The person who tolerates the quizzing prior to the search consultant's offering information may seem weak or hungry rather than confident and gainfully employed.

The executive who receives a cold call pitching him on an assignment has every right to get more information before he reveals more; an exchange, however, is fair. And if called because one has mailed a resume to a search firm, handle the situation in the same fashion. Headhunters, representing the thinking of their client companies, respect pride and confidence. If it appears that a recruiter is reversing the process, *politely* tell him that details about yourself will readily be provided, but more information is needed in order for you to decide if you want to pursue the matter.

There are legitimate instances when the consultant cannot divulge the client's name during the first meeting with an executive. His client has sought anonymity for certain reasons. (However, in fairness to the potential candidate, most headhunters will give some parameters—for instance, the industry the company is in, assets, staff size, and general location.) Reasons for anonymity can include an incumbent in the position who is not aware that his replacement is being sought—typically due to his failure in the job. A company may not want its competitors to know that a key person is leaving, until they hire a strong replacement, as it could hurt their standing in the market. And news of the promotion of a senior executive, without immediately introducing an acceptable replacement, could cause some staff members un-necessary stress. So a search is done without mentioning the client until the headhunter finds Mr. Right.

## THE INTERVIEW WITH A HEADHUNTER/WRITING YOUR RESUME

Assuming you're interested in the position and the company de-scribed, it is now time for the headhunter to interview you—to ask questions regarding your background in order to further qual-ify you. While doing so, the consultant takes notes from which he will build a resume. It pays to have an updated one that can now be given to the recruiter. It saves both parties time. The search consultant can now review the highlights and gather ad-ditional information without having to ask basic questions. You are also spared the strain of having to recall dates of employ-ment, dates when promoted, key achievements, and so on.

As previously mentioned, having a resume doesn't mean an executive is desperate for a job change. It is professional, a sign of being prepared and of being receptive to hearing about a good opportunity. A resume isn't mandatory, just useful. Very senior level officers often won't have one; likewise, people who have been with a firm 20 or more years and who never or very rarely contemplate leaving. However, they may have a public relations piece which their company has prepared about them. They should offer it to the consultant. It can help him better assess and present you to a client, as can select magazine and newspaper articles. The headhunter will write a resume about you even if you have your own. There are always additional points to in-clude, or exclude, in relation to the position in question. Some search firms may also provide clients with a page about the per-sonal style and manner of the candidate.

Infrequently, a headhunter is asked by the candidate for a copy of the resume which he will write. It is the general practice not to do this although some comply. It is an unnecessary extra step for them, an editorial infringement on their professionalism, and one wonders if the resume is sought for review or future use. To the candidate who may be worried that the headhunter may have omitted or misrepresented elements in his background, it is worth noting again that most come out of the fields they're now doing search work in.

The interview styles of headhunters vary as do the durations (about a one hour average) and the types of resumes which they write. They will most certainly inquire about your current and past responsibilities and accomplishments, and probe in this area. When a resume isn't provided, your current and past titles will be asked for, the department or divisions in which you work and have worked, approximate dates at each, size of staff and budget managed, and annual revenues. In addition, inquiries are typically made regarding reporting relationships (often with names), education, military experience, professional activities outside work, the quality of one's references, and why you would consider leaving your present employment. An acceptable and generally truthful reply to this last question could also include the opportunity and challenge just presented, and the additional compensation. The implication is that you are otherwise quite satisfied although open to hearing about advancement. Don't be too hard on your company or management even if you despise them and with good reason. Headhunters can't always tell if you are simply a negative type, being eased out due to failure, or if your employer is at fault—and first impressions are very important. Details about one's reasons for leaving aren't mandatory. But don't lie, particularly if you are being canned, unless your management is covering for you. If you become a finalist candidate, your references will be checked.

Some interviewers ask about your current job and proceed backwards while others prefer to start at the beginning. Some let the candidate begin where he is most comfortable. When a resume is furnished, the recruiter may jump around with questions because the fundamental material is already available. You may make inquiries at any point during the interview.

There are certain illegal questions which are occasionally asked and only you can decide if you care to answer them: age, marital status, size of family, and less frequently, national origin and religion. You don't hear about discrimination suits in the search field. To sue would be an admission that the executive was considering another job. What if his employer found out?

There may be confidential and legal aspects about your position and company which cannot be divulged. Explain this to the interviewer. He will most likely avoid the issues. Similarly, you may feel uncomfortable about telling him the name of the person you work for or your compensation. The former can be initially done without, if you prefer, but a ballpark sense of earnings helps qualify you. The situation may not progress if you don't give him at least a rough idea. Full disclosure is generally required including base salary, bonus, stock options, and perks.

What if a headhunter wants to check a work reference by talking to a past or present manager, but you fear this could jeopardize your current position? Be honest—explain to the headhunter and he will most likely back off. What if he then suggests referencing a trusted customer or former colleague who may even have left an old employer as you have? It strengthens your chances if the information can be obtained, but if it is potentially dangerous, avoid it. The recruiter should understand, especially at this early stage.

The *closing* of an interview is generally initiated by the recruiter. He will usually wind up by saying, "I've gotten all the background I need. Let me mull things over. We both have some thinking to do. I also have a few more candidates to see." Not positive. Or, "I'm interested. How do you feel about the situation?" Positive. Or, "You are definitely a candidate. There are one or two others, but you are in the loop." Positive but not number one.

## THE FOLLOW-UP STAGE

You needn't send a letter to the headhunter telling him how much you simply adored the wonderful time spent together. This is platitudinous and a hunger sign. If you can relate to something unique about the position or the prospective employer that didn't emerge during your visit, then a note adds value. It is not a necessity. The ground can also be covered in a follow-up telephone call. However, if the consultant did something special for you (perhaps he agreed to courtesy interview your spouse or a friend), then a letter is appropriate.

It may take anywhere from a few days to a few weeks before you will hear from the headhunter again. The headhunter may not have enough candidates to refer (three or more are usually gathered before presenting to a client), or the client is away.

When he calls, he may say he is ready to refer you to his client. You naturally indicate your interest. You may, if curious, ask how many have been referred and where you stand. (The headhunter is in a better position to answer the latter after you visit the client—who really has the final say.)

The consultant may call to say—sorry but things didn't work out. Sure, you can ask why. Whether you agree or not, keep him as a friend because there will be other searches.

What if a few weeks or more go by and one hasn't heard? Call and inquire.

So you call back but he's not there. You leave a message yet he doesn't call back. Did he get it? Is he just busy or rude or both? The cold, impersonal, too often exercised rule of business is, not being called back means no interest. But if you are dying with curiosity, hoping beyond reason, and masochistically obsessed with the need for a definite answer—then call. However, some recruiters have their secretaries say they're in Outer Slabovia on a business trip or in an important meeting. You may become more frustrated when your second call isn't answered by these unprofessional types.

However, not returning phone calls is a two-way street.

---

A consultant met with a senior executive from a Fortune 500 company as a courtesy, at the request of a gentleman whom he had placed with a client. He spent an hour with the executive reviewing his resume, answering questions, and giving advice. He even referred him to another client for an exploratory discussion. When he subsequently telephoned the man, his secretary said he was out, but she would have him call back. Two days later, not having heard from the executive, he called again. The secretary assured him that her boss had received the first message and that she would remind him to call. The consultant never heard from him. He checked with his client who confirmed a pleasant meeting. A year later, this executive's company moved their offices into the headhunter's building—and onto his elevator bank. Initially surprised when he recognized the recruiter, this fellow learned to stare intently at the elevator floor readings when they chanced to meet.

---

A few weeks go by, the headhunter calls wanting to refer you, and you are no longer interested. Best to say so rather than duck his calls. He may ask if you know of a possible candidate. Help if you can.

_____ CHAPTER 9 __

# Handling the First Meeting with a Prospective Employer

Despite a candidate's best efforts, not all ostensibly simple first meetings with a prospective employer are, in fact, simple.

---

The headhunter arranged an 8:00 A.M. breakfast meeting for his client and candidate at New York's Intercontinental Hotel, which was near the offices of both executives. Since they had never met, he provided each with a description of the other. He also set up the introduction in an area adjacent to the dining room and hard to miss—a circular lounge

97

under a large parrot cage which was filled with colorful, loudly squawking birds.

The candidate's infant awoke at 3:00 A.M. that morning and cried so intensely that she woke him despite his wife's ministering to the child's needs. At 5:30 A.M., his alarm rang and he rushed through his shower and shave in order to catch the 6:30 A.M. train that would get him into Grand Central Station by 7:45 A.M. Unfortunately, the family dog had gotten sick on the living-room rug. Cleaning it up prevented him from having his morning wake-up coffee. When he arrived at the hotel, he was sluggish, slightly grumpy and had a mild headache. After a few minutes of parrot serenade, he was in a foul mood and his temples throbbed. But he dared not leave the appointed spot lest he miss connecting with the senior executive who could become his new employer.

## THE APPOINTMENT

Headhunters generally find out when you are available to meet with their client (days and times) or tell you when they are available and then arrange a mutually convenient appointment. Be flexible. You may be seeing more than one executive in the company and therefore several schedules may be adjusted to accommodate you. Or you may be seeing a very senior and busy executive. The "they called me" attitude and they have to fit into my schedule won't win you points. If an early morning appointment or a breakfast meeting is scheduled, don't ask the consultant for a wake-up call! Nine out of ten times you won't get it, or a referral.

Cancellations can occur on both sides, but more than one by the candidate can offend and possibly cost you an opportunity. The more senior and successful you are—and the greater the client's appetite for your skills—the more you can get away with it. But for every candidate who cancelled a few times and was rescheduled there is another who was dropped by the prospective employer. It's viewed as waffling and ambivalent or ego-tripping. And not as unexpectedly busy, hardworking, or loyal.

---

The candidate's first appointment was cancelled because he said he was ill. He called the headhunter to cancel the second due to an emergency at work. The recruiter asked, "Are you really interested in exploring the situation?" The executive shot back, "Are they really interested in me?" The dialogue was reported to the client. Despite qualifications which in resume form had sparked the client's initial interest, they had the consultant reject the candidate.

---

The amount of time you spend with the company and whom you will see therein will all be coordinated in advance by the headhunter. If the company ideally wants to see you for three hours and you can only spare two, set this up beforehand. Perhaps two short visits are better for you instead of one long visit.

Lateness without a brief and sincere apology and explanation has also cost candidates jobs. Some say nothing. They treat the lateness with denial as if it never occurred—you invited me; I'm a star so wait for me. Some explain in an indifferent manner.

A candidate who had excellent qualifications sincerely told an executive vice president that he allowed sufficient travel time, but got stuck in traffic on the FDR Drive. He received an abridged interview because it was felt that he didn't allow enough time—anyone in New York knows that the FDR Drive is often congested at peak hours. The candidate showed poor planning and a lack of true interest in the position, according to the strong-minded and decisive senior executive.

Another executive called the company from JFK Airport where he had arrived an hour late. The flight was beyond his control and he did the right thing.

Meetings are generally held at the client's office, but they can also take place in restaurants, clubs, airports, and even a limousine ride when two hectic schedules allow little else.

Needless to say, *standing up a client* is unnecessarily rude (and fortunately happens very rarely). An investment banker, who had been a former candidate of a search firm, where he came in second, was invited to lunch to discuss another position. He was qualified and indicated his interest. An appointment was set up for him to meet the client's European head when the gentleman came to the United States. The appointment was reconfirmed the day prior to the occurrence, in part because the senior executive was on a tight schedule. The candidate didn't show up or call to cancel! Over the next two days, the headhunter called him twice, but received no return call. Was the man embarrassed about forgetting the appointment and neglecting to cancel, perhaps because he grew busy and lost interest? Was he foolish, pompous, or callous? The search firm and the client would never deal with him again—as a candidate or a businessman. They were well connected people and certainly wouldn't praise the investment banker should his name come up.

Recruiters will cover all of your expenses, particularly when they bring you in from out of town to meet their client. The situation is handled in a manner similar to that previously described when the headhunter brings you into his city. Very senior or well-known executive candidates may fly in a company's private jet or first class accommodations; limousines and suites are provided as compared to economy or business class flights, taxis and otherwise nice rooms enjoyed by middle to upper middle management.

## THE HEADHUNTER BRIEFS AND PREPARES YOU

The headhunter will have given you a briefing regarding the company and the executives whom you will meet in preparation for your visit. An annual report probably will have been provided and possibly other materials. He may reiterate or expand on a few points. This is often done subsequent to your initial visit, over the telephone, if not in person. A good recruiter won't insult your intelligence by programming your replies to a client—if the company asks you "this," they want to hear "that." Nor would he be dishonest to a client by behaving this way. The headhunter coaches; he doesn't direct. He naturally wants a placement—but a good one. The consultant aspires to repeat business and a poor placement jeopardizes that.

What if you want more information, what do you do? Ask the headhunter. He may have it or he is able to obtain it more easily than you—a 10K report, a proxy statement, old annual reports, clippings, and so forth. The 10K report will tell you where the company owes money, while a proxy statement (if the company is publicly held) will tell you how many shares key officers have and their incomes. Otherwise, for a fee, you can obtain copies of 10K reports, annual reports, proxy statements and more regarding publicly held companies by calling Disclosure Incorporated at their toll free number (800) 638-8241.

You can also check out a company and its management by talking to someone who works there or who formerly did—and possibly for or with your prospective manager.

## USING DIRECTORIES

Additionally, there are select directories which are readily available in a business library and offer useful insights into companies and their management. Only a few of the very key ones are highlighted here. The more you know about a company and the people whom you are about to meet, the more impressed with you they will be. You were interested enough to find out about them. The information can help you determine if you want to work with them.

*Standard & Poor's Register of Corporations.*   Lists thousands of primarily U.S. corporations, their products and services, key executives, annual sales, number of employees, and so forth.

*Standard & Poor's Register of Directors and Executives.*   Alphabetically lists thousands of executives including their business affiliations, titles, business and home addresses, dates of birth, colleges, and so forth.

*Standard & Poor's Register of Indexes.*   Identifies parent/ subsidiary relationships or which company owns which; also includes companies listed by their industry classification, their location, and so forth.

*Dun & Bradstreet Million Dollar Directory.*   Lists thousands of U.S. companies with net worth over $500,000, including privately owned ones. Information content similar to S&P's *Corporations* volume.

*Dun & Bradstreet Reference Book of Corporate Managements.*   Alphabetically lists thousands of executives with a small resume on them. Similar to Standard & Poor's *Directors and Executives* volume, but offers more information.

*Dun & Bradstreet Principal International Businesses.* Contains information on the world's top 50,000 companies.

*Moody's International Manual, Moody's Bank and Finance Manual,* and *Moody's Transportation Manual.*   Provides information about respective corporations in great depth including their histories and key executives.

*Moody's News Reports.*   Provides periodic updated news about different companies.

*The Value Line Investment Survey.*   Offers a current assessment of a company.

*Who's Who.*   Is a series of volumes in different categories, such as: by geographic location—in America, in the East, West; in different industries—government, finance, and industry; among blacks; among women; and so on; mini-resumes of renowned people.

*Directory of Corporate Affiliations.*   Lists which companies own which and gives greater detail than Standard & Poor's indexes.

*Ward's Directory of 49,000 Private U.S. Companies.* Provides basic information about privately held U.S. firms.

*The Directory of Directories.*   Contains information about innumerable directories which are listed by subject and title.

*The Encyclopedia of Associations.*   Lists thousands of nonprofit American organizations of national scope (trade, professional, union, etc.) and someone who can be telephoned regarding information.

*Reader's Guide to Periodical Literature.*   Is a cumulative index to periodicals (by author and subject) published in the United States.

Each field—law, banking, insurance, corporate finance, security dealers, and so on—has its own directory.


## THE INTERVIEW

Thus, mentally prepared, emotionally ready, professionally attuned (other cares and worries put aside), and properly attired—you arrive for your first interview. Your style and manner should be natural and consistent though you may meet with different executives.

What can you expect during the first visit? What kinds of questions will they ask? What are they after? Expect to be treated courteously and professionally. If for some strange reason you are not—write the place off.

An accountant was kept waiting 45 minutes by the director of a hospital who flew him in from out of town. The director dashed by once, looked at him as if he knew who he was, but said nothing. Later, during the interview, the director seemed grumpy. He never fully excused his lateness. Despite the accountant's gut telling him otherwise, he accepted the position and lived to regret it.

Be wary of the rushed, those who take several telephone calls during your visit, and individuals who speak in their native tongue (a foreign language to you) to colleagues present—unless they excuse themselves.

Expect to initially be given a sense and picture of the company, which may vary slightly depending on the personality and professional discipline of each executive you meet. They will generally offer information and be open to questions. They are, in part, selling—you on them. Personnel may give you an orientation and a broad view of the firm. Your prospective manager may be much more specific and deal with the nitty-gritty of the job. His manager may describe elements of both.

And they will also ask all kinds of questions about you in order to determine your "technical" suitability—does he have the experience and intelligence to do the job. All the while, management is considering "chemistry." Can he fit in with us? Much that the headhunter asked will be repeated and in more depth, and the executives will also repeat themselves (during your separate meetings with them) and ask similar questions.

You can anticipate many of the company's questions:

What do you see as the key elements in this position?

What specific experience do you have to qualify for the job?

Why do you want this post?

How do you propose to help/improve/increase productivity here?

What are your strong and weak points?

What are your achievements/successes on your assignments?

How did you go about accomplishing these goals?

What have you liked and disliked about your positions?

What do your management/clients/peers think of you?

Why did you leave each of your former positions?

What did you basically do in each of your past jobs?

The interview is not a grilling. It is usually fairly relaxed on the surface with a lot of questions and answers from both sides. Prospective employers may ask questions in a sequential fashion, reviewing your resume (as prepared by the headhunter) chronologically. Or they may inquire about particular points that interest them and therefore jump back and forth. You may meet one person or several on a first visit, and they may do any or all of the previously discussed material.

## CANDIDATE FEEDBACK

Candidate feedback encompasses a diversity of experiences after the first visit with the company.

"He did all the talking. I had to interrupt in order to tell him something about myself. He seemed to be selling me on the job without trying to find out about me."

Conversely, one particular president is known to follow a warm greeting with 15 to 30 minute interviews during which he intensely probes candidates. He won't allow questions while he's digging, but he'll make time when he's satisfied. He doesn't sell the job or his company. If he decides you're right for them, he leaves the rest up to his senior management.

Occasionally, executives will ask illegal questions of a candidate. Whether naive or nervy, you can politely tell them the score.

A female vice president candidate for a director of human resources position was asked her height and weight—"for our files," said the interviewer. She flatly refused, quoted the law and the talk ended. She didn't sue; she didn't get the job.

Another individual was asked his religion and gave the information to an executive who had won his trust during a two hour luncheon interview. "I was annoyed with myself later for answering the question. He was a very disarming guy." He didn't get the position.

---

"Throughout the conversation, the General Manager stared at my wristwatch. Our eyes would meet occasionally and very briefly, then he'd drop his gaze to my watch. Was he bored or rushed and checking the amount of time he had? I came so well recommended by you and by his senior staff. What went wrong?" When the headhunter queried the client he was told that the candidate was wearing a $10,000 gold Rolex. The general manager felt that anyone who could afford one wouldn't be motivated enough to do the job. And, unrealistic as this idea might be, the recruiter couldn't disabuse his client of this notion.

---

Be careful about being overly critical of the headhunter's client. Of course, if the company was awful and you're not interested in them, that's another story—though it's rare. You may not know how deep the ties between the headhunter and his client are, and he may believe them and not you. So if you're interested, but had some problem with the company, explain it tactfully. The headhunter will be concerned about hurting his client relationship and also fear a placement who could leave prematurely. But it may be a new client or there may be a known executive who has an unpleasant reputation. Therefore share your experiences.

A headhunter arranged for a long-standing client to fly from New York to Houston and to interview several people whom he had already screened. The senior vice president was to be telephoned from his hotel lobby and candidates would then be invited up to his suite. One executive stood him up, although a note was delivered from the front desk indicating that he had tried to reach him. The senior vice president was firm in saying that he had always been in the room and never on the telephone save for a very brief chat with an arriving candidate. Whom would you believe? Did the candidate call the wrong room? Did he not show up, but called the hotel and left a message to cover himself? Why should the client lie? The candidate was dropped.

An aggressive, senior level financial manager returned from a visit to a long-standing client of the headhunter. Of the personnel manager, whom the recruiter liked a lot, the man had negative things to say. "He's a typical personnel type who doesn't know the job well so he asks simple, obvious questions." The personnel man reported to the president who valued his input about people and used him as a barometer and personal matchmaker for the company. Intuitively, this gentleman had detected a minor unpleasant quality in the candidate's delivery and, later, asked the headhunter if he had noticed it. The candidate was dropped.

You will meet all kinds of people when referred to a company and only you can decide whom you are comfortable with. But a visit is a two-way street—you're sizing them up too, so ask virtually any and all questions that you want to. It's the only way you'll get firsthand information about the company and its people. It is advisable, however, to focus questions during a first visit on the company, its people and the job's content. You may not get all the depth that you need. It will come with subsequent visits. Avoid questions about compensation and benefits. Assume that the headhunter gave you accurate information. This will be explored in later visits.

Infrequently, your first meeting with the company will include the headhunter's presence. There are executives who prefer that he be there to guide the interview. It's atypical, but not inappropriate. And it can work to your advantage because a known entity—the consultant—can take the newness or strain out of the first meeting and even guide it.

It can be exhausting—a visit with several executives, being "on" for hours, extending your best foot. You may need to allow several hours, occasionally days, to digest and code all that has happened. You may find that executives whom you met know people whom you know, and now you want to check with these men and women. Of course, many candidates come away with sufficient interest to quickly know that they would welcome a second visit. Things looked good and another visit is needed to fully determine if the deal is right. Sometimes candidates and companies are sufficiently sure of their interest or lack of it and share this directly with one another. More often, facts are gathered on both sides in a congenial atmosphere. Parties then ask to sleep on it and get back via the headhunter.

## FOLLOW UP

The headhunter will call you later in the day or the next to follow up and see how things went. You should be reasonably candid because he'll work with you in trying to determine if the fit is good on both sides. Typically, he'll call you first, then report to his client. Then he'll get their impressions and get back to you. Positive and negative issues and points are discussed with his clients and candidates. It still may be possible to make the situation work if the company can do "this" or if the candidate will do "that." Give and take—the benchmark of true search—is what goes on, generally, on both sides. There is many a "peg-in-the-hole." But the beauty of this field is that companies needing executives often find them by custom fitting positions to meet their own needs and those of the candidates.

A vice president/sales manager candidate for a consumer goods company liked the company, the executive team and the assignment, with the exception of the territory, which he found to be limited. The company liked him best of the four candidates they had seen on first visits. The consultant suggested to his client that perhaps they could either entice him with more money, expand the territory, or transfer an internal sales manager and offer his territory to the candidate. The company continued its dialogue with the candidate by offering a sign-on bonus, a guaranteed bonus in year one, and a probable change of territory in year two or three, and the candidate accepted the position with these "sweeteners."

A senior vice president/operations manager candidate for a giant western European bank's U.S. activities found the position to be a lateral move in terms of responsibilities. The institution planned to fold the data processing and management information systems area under an ideal candidate in six months, after he grew comfortable with his new job. This individual was very competent in the area and wanted the duties immediately, if he was to go forward as a final candidate. Furthermore, he found the job to be underpriced after gaining more input regarding management's aims during his first visit. The recruiter conveyed all of this to his client while underscoring the man's genuine interest, and also offering a fine personal reference obtained from someone they both knew. The bank granted him his request.

One of the top hundred world banks wanted to hire a union official to market banking services to his industry. The only way to get a foot in the door, they believed, was to attract someone from a union, and they also wanted an aggressive young Turk who wouldn't be put off by countless rejections. They would teach him their products and services. After presenting a handful of appropriate people, the recruiter was told that the client still had not seen the ideal person. The headhunter then presented an unusual candidate. He was a semiretired, senior union executive who also had made a small fortune playing the stock market, had written and published several books—and now only wanted a part-time job. "I don't need the money. I just need something to keep me busy." Of course, the client initially didn't want to even see the man. But the recruiter impressed upon them that his candidate would be more valuable than their original focus. The company eventually hired the man and a junior person to be trained by him.

The headhunter emerges as a mediator, rabbi, and ombudsman in the process. He listens to the needs of both sides and may try to negotiate a mutual fit. His intermediary advisory role to client and candidate requires this even though his first loyalty is to his client. He balances a manageable situation by sharing certain confidences with each.

How forthright will the headhunter be with you in relaying the full results of your visit with a company? It varies from recruiter to recruiter, but most will tell you if the company liked you or if they aren't interested, and why. In either case, feel free to ask the headhunter for details. Some will give you useful input. Sometimes it's hard for them because they can't betray certain client confidences or they think you may not really be receptive to the hard facts, particularly when a rejection is involved.

---

"Why didn't I get the job?" asked the former candidate. "The client liked you," said the consultant, "but they felt you weren't aggressive enough." Shortly thereafter, the consultant got an annoyed call from his client. "Guess who just bit my head off?"

---

An executive and his family had been living in Chicago for the past few years and wanted to return to their hometown, Louisville. He took a temporary consulting assignment in Louisville, was living with his elderly mother, looking for a permanent situation and commuting to Chicago on most weekends. With the aid of a search firm, he became a candidate for a position as division manager. The headhunter called to discuss the status. "Good morning, is Mr. Jones in?" "Good morning," replied his mother in a deep southern voice. "He'll be back later." "O.K., I'll call again." "Excuse me, are you that search fella?" "Yes." "Is my son going to get the job?" "I can't tell yet." "You mean, you can't even tell his little ole mother?"

---

You may be the only candidate, the lead, or one of a few. Some headhunters will tell you this, others won't. They may not want you to get too cocky and possibly demanding should you discover that you're "the one" very early in the search. But by keeping you Mr. Inside Track means there's still a race in progress. So you're less likely to start asking for the moon.

What if several days go by and you haven't heard from the headhunter after the first visit? Maybe the headhunter or his client were away or busy. Call him, if you're interested in the job. He may have gotten negative feedback from his client and there is no interest on their behalf. Nevertheless, it is rude not to offer follow-up or feedback. It's rare that this would happen.

What if you hear from the recruiter after the first visit, he tells you you're a candidate, then you don't hear from him for weeks? You may have been bumped by another candidate, or again, the headhunter and client are busy and things are dragging. The company may be seeing more people. They often will even if they find Mr. Very Good early on. The headhunter should have called you with information. Call him and ask what's doing, if you're still interested. You may, believe it or not, still be in the running, although odds are you're not.

What if you're interested and the client no longer is? There is probably little that can be done to turn things around. You had your chance, but it didn't work out. Perhaps you can convey new information to the headhunter which can be relayed to the company. But it may be fruitless because you lack certain required skills and experiences or the chemistry was lacking. There is plenty of competition out there. An executive may think his credentials are perfect and will qualify him for anything. In reality there are other gifted people around.

It isn't cricket to go around the headhunter and aggressively call the company. Although, if you had a good rapport and you have something special to say it couldn't hurt. A letter presenting additional relevant points can be sent—preceding a call.

A vice president of a firm in New York was asked to relocate to his company's headquarters in San Francisco. Because he was divorced and his children lived with his former wife in New York, he decided to look for another job locally. He interviewed for a particular position and was told he lacked background in certain areas and was rejected. Really wanting the job, he then wrote an exceptional letter outlining why he should be hired—his strengths, weaknesses which were offset by other pluses, and why he had a fervent desire to work with this firm. Management was impressed and flattered by his interest in them. He followed up with a call seeking a second visit. They took another look and they hired him. But this was a rare situation.

What if you aren't at all interested in the position, though you like the company and its people, and they want you? Discuss this with the headhunter. In most cases probably nothing can be done, but he may talk with his client and see what alternatives exist. They may create or find another post for you. They may keep you in mind for the future.

A senior vice president interviewed with the president of a company concerning the top spot in their domestic sales operation. The candidate had domestic and international experience. The initial attraction was the company's reputation and a higher compensation package. However, the job's content ultimately seemed less so he declined a second interview even though he and the president had hit it off. The president, in conversation with the consultant, discussed creating a position for the executive. He would be assigned diverse projects for a year or more and in so doing would learn about the company. Then he would take over the combined domestic and international sales activities.

A senior level leasing executive was shown to a client, but was deemed too strong for the assignment in question. A year and a half later, they called him back and he was hired to manage a larger function.

Last but not least, what if you are interested in the situation and the company is interested in you? Perhaps mutual interest was expressed during your visit with the company and later in dialogue with the recruiter. The recruiter will set up more meetings for you with the company—to meet different executives and spend more time with some whom you've already met.

CHAPTER 10 __

# Subsequent Meetings—
# Dealing with an Offer

The headhunter had set up several meetings between his candidate and the company. They were very interested in each other. A final interview was arranged at the president's club where after dinner, brandy, and cigars, the chief operating officer said, "We'd like to have you join us. What do you say?" The flattered executive replied, "I'd be delighted to." "Excellent," said the president, extending his hand and firmly shaking the other man's. "I'll be leaving the country on Friday morning," he added, "and for a 3-week period I won't be easily reachable. Let me get back to you with a package before I go." Having heard nothing by late Thursday afternoon, the executive called the headhunter to see if he'd heard anything. He hadn't, but he assured the executive that he would call the president and make inquiries. The man heard nothing more from either the recruiter or the chief operating officer that day. On Friday morning at 6:15 A.M. and while he was showering, the telephone rang. The executive ran to the telephone dripping wet, anticipating an emergency. "It's me," said the president, with airport noise in the background. "Sorry to call you at the last minute, but it has been hectic wrapping things up before I depart. I'd like to offer you the following," and he outlined a compensation package somewhat less than was anticipated. The executive began to shiver. The chief operating officer said, "What do you say?" The man wanted the job and realized he was in no position to negotiate, unless he was willing to wait 3 weeks—which he was not.

## SUBSEQUENT MEETINGS WITH THE COMPANY

What can you generally anticipate in subsequent visits with the company? You will meet more senior people. There will be repeat visits with certain key executives—in particular your manager-to-be. They will continue to assess and ask you questions, and you will be doing the same. The more thorough the company, the bigger the job—the more visits you will have and the more senior the management you will meet, including possibly the chairman and some members of the board of directors. The greater your exposure—the easier it is for you to determine how well you might fit in with the company, the job, and the staff. Throughout, the consultant is a go-between coordinating visits, asking the delicate questions of the company for you, sharing their thoughts about you, helping to bring you both closer, and the deal together. One may visit a company three, six or even a dozen times. . . .

The executive had visited with management on a few occasions, then returned for another meeting. The secretary apologetically told him, "Mr. Jones was unexpectedly called away at the last minute. But," she added, "since you are here, I was planning to have lunch with Sara Collins, our office manager. Please join us and be our guest." Fortunately, he accepted and was very congenial. Unbeknownst to him or the headhunter, the company had deliberately set up this ploy. Management wanted a man who got along well with women.

He met all of the company's senior management during the course of many visits. They described him as feisty, hard drinking, pugnacious, brilliant, creative, one-of-a-kind. The evening prior to his morning meeting with the president of the company, the headhunter took him to dinner in order to review the situation. It was a snowy, cold Chicago night. When they left the restaurant, there was 6 inches of snow on the ground. As they walked to the consultant's car, the candidate slipped, fell, and banged his face on the fender. He showed up for his appointment with his face cut and bruised as though he'd been in a fight. Despite the consultant's explanations, that the accident was one that could have happened to anyone, and that the executive had been completely sober, he was rejected by the chief operating officer.

Try to avoid meeting a prospective employer in a place frequented by your management. This can be difficult as restaurants and clubs could unexpectedly have one of them as a patron. Thankfully, only one such experience sadly comes to mind.

A vice president in the private placement field had a third meeting with a major insurance company at the club of one of its top officers. The candidate was one of two finalists. While dining, the vice president's boss emerged from nowhere and came over to his table. Placing his arm around the younger man's shoulder, he said: "See me when you get back to the office."

The poor fellow was given a month's notice by his boss, who reacted as if he had found his wife in bed with another man. And the vice president didn't even get the other job.

Fortunately, most situations move along predictably. There is a continued meeting of the minds and a give and take on behalf of the candidate and company. The candidate may want more responsibility, an additional support person or two whom he believes is lacking on his new team, more money or added perks, another territory, and so forth. Often using the consultant as a liaison, these requests are negotiated in ongoing visits. An offer is eventually made or the recruiter tells you that the other finalist won.

There are, however, certain corporate or individual executive practices and requests that may develop during a candidate's future meetings. Some are not uncommon; some are quite rare. Most are generally considered acceptable corporate behavior although some candidates may justifiably balk—even if it costs them a top job. In no particular order, here are some possible requirements.

1. Meeting the finalist's wife, usually over dinner with her husband, or at a social gathering. Why? You work long and hard—is she behind you? Behind every good man. . . . It's also another way to judge you. Furthermore, homogeneity is sought in some companies; they don't want a possible nudist who's into body tatoos. A warm, team bond can sometimes be established be-

tween the men and women. The practice is quite common, particularly in senior level recruiting. It could mean that the candidate and spouse are flown to another city or country to meet with senior management.

2. The presentation of a plan regarding how you would handle the assignment. It was asked of three semifinalists for the presidency of a to-be-formed trust division, in a worldwide financial institution. All complied. One was late; another too theoretical. The winner was brief, practical and to the point.

3. Taking psychological and aptitude tests given by an outside clinical or industrial psychologist. This is infrequently requested by a client. The finalist for executive vice president and chief financial officer for a medium-sized company in the southeast was being recruited from a large mid-west firm where he was the number two man in finance. Would he fit in from a personality and cultural perspective? Was he bright enough and strong enough for the number one spot? The new owners were replacing several key, senior managers and wanted to be absolutely sure, even if hiring ostensibly successful people who performed basically the same job in a similar company. Their attitude was, why not use all the tools at our disposal? A successful semifinalist who hated tests and felt he was beyond this, declined to go on.

4. A lie detector test was requested by a jewelry and leather goods manufacturer as a preemployment requirement. It's rare, but the executive in question complied. He got the job.

5. A written test was designed by the personnel director of a European company for all U.S. candidates whom he felt might have potential for a chief accountant post in New York. It was composed of 15 essay questions. He administered it by leaving candidates in an empty room, with pad and pen for an hour. Of three candidates presented, surprisingly, all were willing to take the test (it was a good position). The headhunter advised his client that this was possibly an illegal procedure in the United States because the test had not been statistically validated and could also be discriminatory. It might also turn off a quality can-

didate. Such testing is a very rare phenomenon. The personnel director continued to insist on the written test.

6. Handwriting analysis (graphology) is very rarely requested. It is not scientifically valid and also poses legal considerations. But clients have requested it and candidates have complied. Two instances come to mind. Both were with old European firms, one privately held and the other government owned, though both were large and worldwide in scope.

---

A presidential candidate for a company's U.S. operations was asked to submit a handwritten paragraph on any subject. The man was the president of a sizable U.S. company, earned over $200,000 yearly, and initially said no. But he was born overseas and as he put it, "I understand the old world mentality of the founder and chairman. I've gone this far. I'll go one more step, even though I don't believe in this." So he wrote a five sentence paragraph summarizing his business achievements. Results came back that he'd written with a felt tip pen and would he do it over. The recruiter spent an hour assuaging the executive who eventually wrote a ball point pen sample. Results came back that he passed, and he was hired.

---

The other client made this request of a vice president level sales candidate. He complied without a blink. The recruiter wondered why. He even thought it was suspicious. Yet he was a quality executive whose references were sterling. Apparently he was more understanding and flexible or else he was hungry for a change.

7. Traveling to the office headquarters, which is often in another city or country, for a final interview and approval by senior management. European banks regularly send senior vice presidents and above level candidates to their home office for a rubber

stamp, top management review. Finalists generally travel business class to London, Paris, Amsterdam, Zurich, and so forth, and stay in top hotels, suffer jet lag, and several hours' difference in time schedules, but have had their adrenaline help them through a few interviews. You may be lucky enough to have a recruiter set up a visit that enables a full night's sleep between your flight and appointments. You'll dine at a fine restaurant or two, but there is rarely any time for sight-seeing.

8. Traveling to the city or country where your potential new job is located—with your spouse—to see if you both would like living there.

A client in Rochester, New York, a cold and drab town known for its heavy snowfalls, flew finalists and spouses up to spend a chaperoned weekend. They met the community's elite, visited the country club, dined at the best restaurants, checked out private schools for their kids, and house hunted. Similar activities occur regarding a Middle East posting. It may take more than one visit to sell an executive and spouse if a less than desirable location is involved.

Sometimes spouses aren't interested in relocating to a given city. It may cause an executive to pass up an offer or if the opportunity is too good to refuse marital separation or worse can result.

An executive earning $125,000 in Atlanta, the number two man in a medium-sized company, was offered the presidency of a bigger firm in a small mid-western city at a salary of $225,000. His wife refused to relocate because she loved the community they lived in, had personal and family ties nearby and liked her job a great deal. Interestingly, their two children were in boarding school and posed no problem in her decision. The executive took the job, relocated, and visited his wife and children most weekends.

A teacher in suburban Philadelphia refused to relocate to New York or its environs despite an exceptional offer that her husband received. She was a third generation Philadelphian and rooted. So he drove a half hour to the train, spent at least an hour riding into New York, and another half hour getting to his Wall Street office by subway and a walk of a few blocks. The commute was a strain on their marriage. He left the position after two years. Yet there are people who have done this for years and survived.

9. Corporate foot dragging—whether to finally hire the executive—is not uncommon. It may occur in select situations or be standard and institutionalized in large corporate environments where one has to be approved up the line—from executive to senior executive. This does not mean that all big companies act slowly. Many move swiftly. Don't necessarily equate slowness with a lack of interest in you. Candidates should therefore have patience. Some get annoyed at the client and the headhunter because of delays. The client's first obligation isn't recruiting. It is keeping the company profitable. This practice also keeps the consultant, as well as the candidates, waiting.

A vice president was introduced by the headhunter, along with three other candidates, for a director of public relations position. The company met the four individuals and decided that the vice president was the best man. So they had him come back to meet the heads of several line functions with whom he'd interface. Their thoroughness, coupled with scheduling difficulties because their management was often away on business trips or vacations, caused the search to drag on for four months. In the interim, the finalist was promoted to first vice president and received a substantial pay hike. The happy ending is that he nevertheless went to work for the new company, but it cost them more than they planned and they had to sell hard in order to finally attract him.

If as a result of subsequent interviews you are eliminated, the headhunter will usually give you an explanation. Otherwise, ask him why you were eliminated. Executive recruiting is very competitive. It's also biased by the subjective style of senior management or the senior executive doing the hiring.

An executive vice president and number two man in a $600 million company, who had a marvelous track record plus a Harvard MBA, was not acceptable to another firm of equal size for their number one spot. The reason: poor grooming—his shoes were scruffy and his hair was too long. He was later placed by the headhunter as president of a larger company for more money.

An executive had several interviews, was well liked by management and was the lead candidate for a position. He then dined with the head of the division, salted his steak before tasting it ("which showed poor judgment"—according to the senior executive) and he wasn't hired.

---

Taking this a step further, the finalist for a division presidency in a major cosmetics company was invited to dine with the chairman at his penthouse. The recruiter met his candidate for a drink and last minute prep talk before he went up. The next day the recruiter called his contact, the personnel director, and asked, "How did it go?"

"He doesn't know how to eat artichokes," was the reply.

"But how did it go?"

"His teeth need fixing."

"All right, but how did it go?"

"The chairman and I laughed when he got up from the sofa because his pants clung to his socks."

"We can teach him how to eat artichokes. We can get his teeth fixed. And we can spray his slacks and make them static free. But can he do the job?"

"Does it matter?"

---

## DROP OUTS

Sometimes the candidate loses interest in the job, the company, or its people, and decides to drop out. Some stop returning telephone calls to the headhunter and client.

The lead candidate for a first vice president and chief trader position stopped returning telephone calls. She was in her early thirties, with degrees from a top Ivy League school, doing a similar job with another financial institution. She was earning a base and bonus of $125,000 annually. The firm seeking her offered a base of $125,000 and a bonus of up to $75,000, including a first year guarantee of $25,000. Finally, the headhunter called late one evening. "Sorry to disturb you at this hour," he said politely, "but I haven't been able to reach you." The woman who had answered said, "You must want my sister. She's not in. I'll tell her you called." "You sound just like her," said the recruiter. There was a moment of silence. Then the woman said, "I'll tell her you called," and hung up. The recruiter never heard from her "sister."

Needless to say, this kind of behavior is unprofessional. Fortunately, it's also uncommon.

Sometimes a company begins getting bad press in the media while a search is in progress and a candidate changes his mind. A company may begin losing money or a few key executives may leave, causing candidates to lose interest. An entire continent, such as Latin America, began suffering financial and political difficulties and many who might have considered employment there were dissuaded.

A major U.S. company was given a franchise by the government of China to build factories in a heavily populated (5 million people) but isolated city. The company retained a headhunter to recruit two executives. A few days later, the headhunter read in the newspaper that there were riots in the city directed at a woman accused of fraud. Many of the residents wanted her executed. Not long after, a follow-up article mentioned that these people had indeed publicly executed her. Several possible candidates read the report of the incidents and withdrew from consideration although the jobs were eventually filled.

An American and his wife were flown to Kuwait by a Fortune 1000 company to see if the locale, housing, and private schools were suitable for them to relocate there. On their third day in the country, the U.S. Embassy was bombed. A week later all U.S. citizens were evacuated. Just as well—the candidate was no longer interested in the job.

---

The finalist candidate and his wife were house hunting in San Francisco and staying at a hotel as guests of his probable new employer. They were scheduled to lunch with the headhunter, but upon arriving at their hotel he found they had unexpectedly checked out and were en route to the airport. He caught up with them as they were boarding. "We won't live in this town," said the executive in a shaky voice. "Last night's earthquake threw us both out of bed."

---

## THE JOB OFFER

If all things continue to look very good on both sides, a job offer is the logical next step. How is the offer made? What can the executive expect in terms of compensation and perks?

The headhunter will usually feel you out prior to the actual offer. He typically will say, "The company wants to offer you the position and they are thinking about a base salary of. . . . The other compensation ingredients will include . . . and the perks are. . . . "

The other compensation ingredients generally include either a bonus, profit sharing, stock, an expense account, a 401K program, and so forth. Perks are clubs, a car, financial consulting, free housing, free schooling, servants, and so forth. Both are generally predetermined by the company for a particular job and are pretty standard within a given industry. This is especially true for middle management positions. There is more negotiation and flexibility regarding compensation and perks with senior positions; there are fewer standards here. For example, it may be necessary to obtain financial consulting, if it's not provided by the new employer, to review the many facets of the offer. You may be getting a higher base salary, but the cost of living in the new city is higher. Perhaps the taxes are too. Also, will the new company buy your house or aid you in resettling? You have to look at the total deal and you may have to negotiate for what you need and want.

---

After several meetings, there was no question in the chairman's mind; he wanted this man to be his president. And the candidate was extremely interested in the post. But they were $25,000 apart. The chairman invited the executive and the consultant to his apartment for dinner and hopefully a closing talk. Drinks, dinner, conversations about opportunities, ways to run the business, common philosophies; however, the executive still wanted more money. "I'll arm wrestle you for it," suggested the host. "You're on," responded his equally macho guest. They rolled up their sleeves, sat down on the thick living room rug, and clasped hands over a $5,000 glass coffee table. Moments into what seemed an equal match, the chairman said, "If the money means that much to you, it's yours." The fate of a major company had been negotiated.

---

The offer should be in keeping with the package the headhunter originally and perhaps subsequently discussed with you. If it seems low, discuss it with him. If anything can be done, he'll help. Approximately 20 percent total cash increases are the standard, middle management offer. More is obtainable in certain fields, if you're really talented, at senior levels, if you're joining a financially troubled company, a start-up operation, where there is a great need, or if you are relocating to a high cost of living city, and so forth.

In the headhunter's original presentation of an assignment, he may say it could pay *up to* $100,000 for the ideal candidate. The finalist, perhaps earning $70,000, may think the upper figure is what he'll be offered. When $85,000 or $90,000 comes along, he's put out. It's up to the headhunter to have prepared him for this, but candidates often lock in on the upper number mistakenly.

The investment banking community is a notoriously good payer. A vice president in mergers and acquisitions with a major firm, who was in his early thirties and earning $500,000 yearly, was offered a $750,000 minimum guarantee for two years and a partnership by a competitor. (He turned it down. He felt he'd make partner in his firm on the next pass in one or two years and that the increased compensation would be eaten away by taxes anyway.)

If you and the consultant come to a mutual understanding about the package, the company will usually then make a more formal offer—in person or over the telephone.

How does the executive handle an offer? Does he simply accept a desirable one, or sleep on it, or negotiate for more money and responsibility? If you like what you are offered—accept it. If there are questions or concerns, discuss them with the headhunter and the company—preferably in that order. The headhunter can aid in further negotiations or with preemployment issues, and leverage for you.

Many accept an offer when it is made because there are no surprises—all has been reviewed previously. Many take it home and sleep on it over the weekend. Now that the job is theirs, they can fully weigh in the reality of leaving what they have and joining a new company. This often happens with satisfied executives whom the recruiter approached rather than executives who were disgruntled and looking. Don't sleep on the offer for too long because it can be rescinded. Discuss your reasons for possibly wanting to extend a decision with the consultant.

As one headhunter used to say to finalists who wanted a week to mull over an offer, "Take your time. Don't take the job unless you're sure you want it. But should you decide not to accept— I've got some friends down at the docks who will be in touch."

Don't tell the company, should they offer what was agreed on between you and the headhunter, that you want more. It could cost you the job. One lucky executive who pulled this stunt was politely told the following by the company, but through the recruiter. "They still want you to join them, but at the original dollars which we discussed. They think you're a tough negotiator, but green to the process. They hope you'll accept, but if you hold out for more money, they'll be forced to hire someone else."

After countless meetings, the presidential candidate for Playboy asked for $2 million . . . and it was accepted. Then after conferring with his lawyers, he asked for $4 million. He was rejected.

A lot more money isn't the most important reason for a move. If there is more opportunity in the new assignment or if you are displeased for whatever reasons where you are employed—weigh these factors against expectations for gargantuan salary hikes.

## EMPLOYMENT CONTRACTS/LETTERS OF UNDERSTANDING

Should the executive seek an employment contract, or a letter of understanding? They obviously can protect you if something happens with the new employer that negatively affects you. For instance, your manager leaves and his promises are not going to be met by his replacement. Attorney-prepared contracts (generally lengthy and phrased in legal terms) are not always granted by companies. They may prefer to use a letter of understanding, which will briefly describe the offer (title and basic responsibilities, compensation, perks, and start date). Generally, the more senior the position, the greater likelihood of your obtaining a contract. Otherwise, they're granted less frequently. Straightforward employment letters are more easily gotten and many companies offer them routinely while others just don't. Your ability to gain a contract is greatly increased in risky situations—joining a financially troubled company or a start-up venture. Herein one can also leverage for a separation clause—if the operation fails, you'll be paid full salary for a period of time (often a year or more).

The final candidate for senior vice president and head of operations with a multibillion dollar company requested a contract. He knew that his predecessor had been terminated after several years in the job and by the new chief operating officer— who made him this offer. The chief operating officer countered that the fired executive had been given six months' severance, outplacement assistance—and all this despite his being incompetent and untrustworthy. He wouldn't offer a contract because he wanted his key managers to trust him as he would them. This element of trust was very important to him. For the executive to go to work without a contract would be an indication of that trust. There were dangers here. If the chief operating officer made promises and then wouldn't keep them for whatever reasons, what recourse did the new man have? If the chief operating officer left the company or was promoted, would his successor honor the pledges? On the other hand, would the candidate get the job if he insisted on a contract? He decided to accept the verbal offer. The chief operating officer then voluntarily gave him a letter delineating most of their arrangement. He had wanted control and an ingredient of trust. Once that was established to his satisfaction, he was willing to come up with the letter of understanding.

If you want a contract or a letter, ask the headhunter about the possibility of getting one. There are certain industries where contracts are more common and often required by the company. In the June 6, 1983 *Forbes* article, "Who Owns Your Brains?," it was pointed out that of the top 100 industrial companies in America, one-third require contracts. And industries which generally require them include the very competitive ones, such as computers, pharmaceuticals, toys, defense equipment, and electronics.

If your prospective employer requires that you sign a contract, have it reviewed by a lawyer before you sign and keep a copy for your reference. You may plan to leave the company in the future and the contract states what you can and can't do. It may have a restrictive covenant which can prevent you from working in your field for a period of time after you leave the company. Several states prohibit this because it prevents one from earning a living. But if your new employer is inflexible regarding this clause, discuss a rider clause with the consultant that will give you full pay during the noncompete time.

## GIVING NOTICE

Let us assume that with the assistance of the headhunter an offer has been made by the company, a package negotiated including dollar ingredients and perks, a contract or letter of understanding may have been provided, and the candidate has accepted. What happens next? The executive gives notice to his present employer, usually to his immediate manager, that he has accepted another position and will be leaving. In instances where a contract or letter is involved, resignations occur either before or after signing. It pays to sign first and give notice after. Why? If the new employer considers changing his mind after you've quit, an unlikely situation, you have a legal document showing that they made an offer and you accepted.

How much notice is appropriate? It hinges on how long you've been with the company, how senior or vital your role is, your rapport with your employer and your desire to do the right thing and not leave too quickly and hurt them and your reference, how quickly your new company wants you, and so forth. It is appropriate to leave a minimum of 2 weeks' notice yet be flexible should your management need more time. Four weeks and possibly more is acceptable for senior people with major responsibilities who are professional about departing. Your company may want to find your replacement before you leave. You may or may not be able to remain that long depending on your arrangement with the new employer.

Some firms, despite your good intentions, will want you out immediately because they fear you may be privy to information which you will use in your new shop. There are a few brokerage firms which are known for locking up a broker's desk when he gives notice—that moment or close to it being his last with the house. They fear the individual will copy customer lists, contact them and try to sway them over to the new company. There is a large international bank that only allows one to stay a few days past notice even if you've been there several years. The logic is similar.

So you set up a departure date with your present employer and subsequently confirm a start date with your new one. Perhaps you can arrange for some vacation time in between. The headhunter will work with you, in trying to carve out a few days or more and act as the go-between with your new employer if necessary. It can be an unfettered time. The old challenge is put to rest and the new one is forthcoming—rest hard while you can.

Throughout these final preemployment stages, the recruiter is in constant touch with the executive, typically by telephone and often in person. He is fine tuning the deal and moving it toward a close. The final needs and wants of both sides are being explored and met. The consultant may dine with his candidate in order to accomplish the aforementioned in a relaxed setting. He is also subtly keeping the pressure on the candidate not to change his mind. It is never blatantly so stated although the headhunter's attentiveness and presence are hand holding a somewhat obligated executive toward the finish line. However, most executives are bright and strong minded enough not to be drawn into the wrong situation. And most recruiters wouldn't allow this to happen.

## REFERENCE CHECKING

One of the executive search consultant's final obligations to his client is to check the to-be-hired executive's references. They are usually checked after an offer is made, accepted, and notice given. All employment offers are made contingent on satisfactory references.

Whom does the headhunter want to talk to about one's references? He usually asks for the name of your current manager and a few former ones from past employment situations. References are generally done over the telephone. What happens if one of your references is poor? Generally they needn't all be sterling as long as the bulk of them are good to very good. Even really good references may have a point regarding an imperfection. It rings false when people offer glowing, superficial praise about you. Discuss potential problems with the consultant long before he checks them. He can be an ally and may be able to act in your behalf. Many people have had a bad experience in certain employment situations. Positive offsetting references or other information may be developed which can temper a negative review. However, a reluctance to divulge reference names is a red flag that you have something to hide. Don't get caught lying about your references. Offers can be rescinded.

The reference issue is a particularly sensitive area. Although most references of senior executives are fine, a few are fraught with: the unexpected, biased opinions, dated evaluations, and dilemmas.

He accepted the new job which involved extensive travel. A reference indicated that he was exceptionally talented and hard working. It also revealed that his wife was an alcoholic, which was possibly due to his previous excessive travel. Should all the information be shared with the client? After much thought, the headhunter told his client. The offer was rescinded.

---

The departing president of a medium-sized firm was the finalist candidate for the presidency of a larger company. He had two excellent references from former situations, but wasn't sure what his current board would say, since he didn't see eye to eye with them. The recruiter sounded out two key board members. One said, "I wouldn't recommend him for any job." The other said, "I don't want to talk about him at all." The consultant was dismayed and upset by the depth of their negative reaction—he had never encountered such excessive hostility before.

He shared his experience with the executive, who suggested that the recruiter talk to his predecessor at the company. When the headhunter did, he learned that this man had gotten the same awful references because, like the candidate, he also didn't agree with the board's policies. He then offered the name of *his* predecessor as a further reference. When the consultant spoke to this other man, he got a very similar story. The headhunter reported all this to the client and the candidate was hired.

---

An old line firm with a very uprighteous image made an offer to a chief operating officer candidate, which he accepted. Prior to giving notice, the executive arranged for the headhunter to make a few discreet reference checks with peers in related companies. Telephone calls yielded reports that the man "ran a profitable company and that he was a real good guy." The consultant felt he was getting superficial information and no depth regarding the man's real nature and character. He therefore tactfully tried a few personal contacts of his own, and got more candid information. He discovered that the candidate was "a womanizer who engaged prostitutes," "an animal and a barbarian when he was on the road," and he was told of an incident at a national sales meeting where he took off with a young woman sales trainee and wasn't seen for 2 days.

Alarmed by the reports, the recruiter informed his client, who agreed to rescind the offer. Rather than confront the executive with their findings, they cooked up a deal. A friend of the consultant's, an outside board member with the candidate at another company, was enlisted. After a meeting, he pulled the candidate aside and said, "You should reconsider the offer you got. The company really isn't doing as well as they suggested. And I've heard other negatives about them from reliable sources." The seed of doubt was planted. When the headhunter called the man a few days later and said, "The company is having second thoughts about hiring you because of financial problems," the executive said, "I'm having second thoughts too." And when the headhunter called again and lamented about the company, he and the finalist agreed it was best to drop the whole thing.

Postscript. A few months later, the press announced that the company had hired a new chief operating officer and for more money than this fellow had been offered.

---

An operations vice president and manager with a large brokerage firm accepted an offer from a competitor. When the consultant approached him regarding references, he said, "We have a problem. I'm not a vice president and operations manager. I'm an assistant vice president and assistant operations manager. But I was expecting the promotion and it was delayed for a few months." The consultant unhappily acknowledged the gray element in the misrepresentation and asked the individual if the salary he presented was still accurate. He was told it was. Relaying all this to his client, the recruiter was asked to verify compensation with an income statement. They were willing to be flexible—after a heart-to-heart talk with the man. When the excited searcher relayed the good news to the executive, the latter said: "We have another problem. I'm not earning that much money. But I'm worth it." The executive search consultant, barely keeping his temper, said, "No one doubted what you are worth, but you certainly claimed to be earning more. Furthermore, you've embarrassed us both with the company." "Well then, let's just forget the whole thing," said the man. Forget? Never. The offer was rescinded.

An executive who lied about his references got a call from the search consultant who rescinded the offer on the client's behalf. The man literally cried over the telephone. Days later, the consultant got a call from the man's wife. "My husband doesn't know I'm talking to you," she said in an upset voice. "Is there something about him I should know?"

One can be hurt by negative references that are not work related.

He accepted an offer, quit his job, and prepared to relocate. Each member of the board at his new employer then got a poison pen letter from a young woman claiming to have been his fiancee. "You shouldn't hire him. He's dishonest. He's married and didn't tell me, and he has several drunk driving arrests." The headhunter called the individual and confronted him. The executive denied it all. He even signed a deposition to that effect prepared by his new employer's attorneys. But the company did a check on him and found two drunk driving arrests. Their private detective proved he was having an affair with the woman and had proposed marriage although he was already married. The company rescinded the offer and the man was left unemployed.

A woman telephoned a headhunter and in a tearful voice told him how his finalist was two-timing her. "He's married and he never told me. And we're engaged. He lives in Miami and regularly travels here on business. That's how we met." The consultant presented the information to the finalist who confessed. He was dropped as a candidate. Weeks later the woman called the headhunter back. "I can't thank you enough for what you did. If my family can ever do you a favor—just ask. We can help, you know. We're very close around here. We took care of him." "What do you mean?" asked the consultant. "We broke his legs." Concerned, the headhunter called the man—he was hospitalized with two broken legs.

---

To avoid getting caught in a squeeze between giving notice and possibly poor references, one very cautious executive made a proposal to the recruiter. He encouraged him to first check his references with a current and past manager, both of whom he felt wouldn't divulge that he was looking for another job. If the references were good, he'd resign; if not, he'd stay put. Of course, the man tipped the headhunter off regarding shaky references. The headhunter relayed all this to his client. Both decided it was appropriate to check his references and then see because the executive had been a very attractive candidate up until this point. The references, surprisingly, were glowing—he was hired.

What can the executive do to maximize the quality of his references? If you've had more than one manager at each of your positions, and one liked you more than the other—give his name as a reference. Keep this in mind during your early conversations with the headhunter. He may benignly ask whom you reported to at each position. This is also true of your interviews with the company. It's not inappropriate to say, "I had more than one manager, but the one who knows me best is. . . . " The wrong name could come back to haunt you. When it's reference time, you can't offer another name—without a very good excuse. You'll look like you're trying to hide something—possibly a bad reference. A good excuse to use just in case you slipped? "I don't know where he moved to after he left the company." Don't say he's with XYZ Company in Paris because the headhunter can call anywhere.

It is also to your advantage to talk to your former managers before your references are checked. You will be able to explain the situation to them. It can enable the headhunter's call to get answered smoothly and promptly. This can have an additional positive effect on the reference—how readily and favorably they remembered you. There will be less likelihood of reluctance on their behalf—about divulging personal information—which can arise when one is referenced unexpectedly and is possibly suspicious and defensive. People who provide references have to be careful because they can be sued for libel.

A vice president, whom the executive recruiter suspected might be homosexual, accepted a new position, but received a vague and generally poor reference from his current manager. He had not started the new job and the information was of concern to the recruiter. Prior to alerting his client, he discussed the reference with the executive. The man then sent a registered letter to his manager, unbeknownst to the recruiter, informing him that if unfairly maligned he would sue, and a better reference was subsequently initiated by the manager. The consultant informed his client of the proceedings and the man was hired.

Setting the stage for the headhunter's call to a former manager can give an indication if he indeed will give you a quality reference. Perhaps he seems reluctant, disinterested, or too busy. It is best to offer the headhunter a supplementary reference if this individual's name has already been presented.

One vice president was so sure his references were excellent that he encouraged the recruiter to call his current and past two superiors without his alerting them first. Two were fine; one was a stab in the back. The executive received the position anyway, but his file with the new employer already included an unnecessary blemish. When he is reviewed for future opportunities in the firm, will that hurt him?

---

A Japanese executive was being considered for a managerial position with a U.S. company in Tokyo. Ten years previously, he had spent a few years in the United States with his firm as a general manager. A reference from a senior level American businessman who had dealt with him was requested. The candidate submitted the names of a few though he had not been in contact with them in many years.

The search consultant was able to track one person down. He was a partner in a consulting firm that had been retained by this executive. He said, "Mr. Kawabata did good work, but I dislike Japs. He had clean and accurate books, but in my book all Japs are Kamikazes. You know his boss was a Kamikaze destroyer commander! I dislike all Japs because of World War II. It was a trying time for me."

It would have been very difficult, though not impossible for Mr. Kawabata to have spoken with this reference prior to giving his name. A good reference from this man was equal to great! The executive was hired.

It is additionally useful if you can tell your references the types of questions that will be asked. Don't ask the headhunter for samples—it may be interpreted as a sign that you have something to hide. What is generally asked is pretty straightforward.

How do you know Mr. Jones and what is his relationship to you?

How long has he worked for you and approximately what are his dates of employment?

What is his title and basic responsibilities?

How would you assess the quality of his work?

Does he manage people and how many?

Is he a good manager?

Does he get along with people—superiors, peers, as well as subordinates?

What are his strengths and weaknesses?

What is his approximate compensation?

Does he manage his personal life and finances satisfactorily?

Why is he leaving your firm?

Would you rehire him?

He's being hired for the position of _____ with responsibilities for _____. Do you think he can handle this?

Is there anything else about him you think we should know?

The offer has been made and accepted. Notice has been given and a starting date arranged. References checked out satisfactorily. All that remains before physically joining the new firm is the last few weeks with your old employer. Right? Perhaps. . . .

## A COUNTER OFFER/ANOTHER OFFER/ A COUNTER-COUNTER OFFER

A counter offer by one's employer or another offer occurring near simultaneously (the executive was interviewing with more than one company) has occasionally caused employment arrangements to fall through. The candidate, in most cases, has genuinely accepted the new job, but gets turned around. Consultants then resurrect the number two or number three candidates, start over, or cry. A counter-counter offer has occurred too. This happens when the executive accepts a new job, is then convinced by his old management to remain, and is finally resold on the idea of moving on by the new employer. It's rare and more likely in new industries where there is less talent.

Just before his employer sent him on a business trip to Europe, a finalist was made an offer and accepted. He accepted a counter offer from his manager while overseas. A month later, he returned and told the headhunter about his decision. The prospective employer lost a month's time as a result. The executive said he'd personally call the company and explain and apologize. The recruiter set the stage. The man never called, further embarrassing the headhunter and hurting his relationship. The number two choice was brought back into the loop and eventually given an offer. He accepted, but was counter offered three days prior to starting the new job (merely his employer's delay or re-venge?). And this was after signing a letter of commitment, which the company did not plan to hold him to. The number three man received the position while in the interim the consultant got gray hair!

Thankfully, circumstances like this do not happen often. And it also points out that the number one or two candidates, the most seemingly qualified, don't always get the job. But when it does occur, most people are gentlemen. As one executive put it, "Thanks for getting me a promotion and a salary raise." One headhunter, however, was informed by letter that the executive was changing his mind—on the Friday prior to his Monday start date.

---

A vice president was made an attractive offer. His reaction was generally positive, but he asked to have the weekend to think about it. By late Monday afternoon, the company called the headhunter because they had not heard from the man. The headhunter called him, but he was told he'd been in meetings all day. The recruiter called him at home that evening and his wife said he'd been forced to work late be-cause of some problem. Tuesday morning the consultant called the candidate, but received no reply. The headhunter was obviously suspecting the worst. That afternoon, the man telephoned and apologized. "I've been so busy; it prevented me from focusing on the offer. Could I please have a few more days to mull it over?" Although the headhunter doubted the veracity of the excuse, there was a note of pos-sible truth. He asked, "Is there anything missing in the offer that you might want to discuss?" But the executive an-swered, "No, I just need more time." The headhunter said, "If it's another situation that you're looking at—let's be open so we can negotiate." The vice president hedged and said, "It isn't another job." All of this was discussed between consultant and client. The company asked the recruiter to call the man back and tell him they really wanted him to join them and that he had until Friday to decide, lest they rescind the offer. He did so. That Friday the finalist called. "I don't quite know how to explain all that has been happening. While I was interviewing with you another search firm called with an interesting opportunity. I really liked both and only recently made up my mind. It wasn't easy. But I'm accepting the other offer. Thank you so much for your assistance. I'm sorry if I caused you any trouble. I hope we can stay in touch—just in case this situation doesn't work out." The headhunter politely told him that, "We would have appreciated your being more candid. We suspected that you had another lead. We were up front with you and were upset that you didn't level with us." The man said, "I was afraid the company would strike the offer if they knew." The headhunter replied, "But we knew by your evasiveness. Furthermore, how could I keep you in mind for other assignments since you might embarrass me again with other clients? It wasn't that you took another job that disturbs me— it was how you conducted yourself."

---

Headhunters realize that executives may be looking at other opportunities. This doesn't anger them though it is upsetting. However, companies rarely retract offers from people they want just because these individuals are weighing in other assignments. They recognize that the talented are in demand.

An executive in the integrated-circuits field accepted a new position. He was then counter offered by his management and decided to stay. The headhunter relayed this to the client who acted swiftly. They flew the executive to their headquarters, introduced him to top management who proverbially opened a check book and said: "Name your price, my son." He joined them.

## THE FUTURE RELATIONSHIP

These negative experiences aside, most executives who accept a position go to work for the company. And what is the future relationship between the executive and the executive recruiter?

Many headhunters take their placements out to a big celebration lunch or dinner at a top restaurant. They can both let their hair down, be jovial, and friendships can develop.

---

The newly hired sales manager was taken to Lutece by the recruiter. As the recruiter dined on his cornish hen, he noticed a small, intact wishbone. Removing it, he then cleaned it on his napkin. "I hope you don't find me crude or superstitious," he said. "But I think this apropos. Care to make a wish?" And he extended one end of the bone while he gripped the bottom of the other piece. The executive immediately complied. They each pulled their piece toward them, and it snapped in the executive's favor. He was so delighted that he took it home as a souvenir.

---

Sometimes the headhunter is fondly remembered by the person he places. He may be asked to do a search for him.

Many executives whom the headhunter places get promoted, a few become millionaires, and a few go on to run the company. Some get headhunted away by other search firms to still bigger posts. Headhunters have a vital role in upgrading executives and increasing their visibility and opportunities.

Korn/Ferry International took the head of a successful travel agency chain and brought him into the public's eye. Peter Ueberroth was placed as the president of the Los Angeles Olympic Organizing Committee for the 1984 summer Olympic games. His achievements were so exceptional that he attracted the attention of others. The search firm of Heidrick and Struggles then placed him as the commissioner of baseball.

# SECTION III

# Corporate Considerations

# CHAPTER 11

# For Companies Planning to Use a Search Firm— Part One

If you are a line manager or a human resources executive and you need to use a search company how do you go about choosing one?

## SELECTING A SEARCH FIRM

Talk to your business friends—inside and outside your company—regarding the firms they use and which ones they like. The concise list of major executive search firms provided in Chapter 6 will be useful, as will the encompassing *Directory of*

*Executive Recruiters* and possibly the more abridged AESC membership list. Line managers may find it helpful to seek counsel with their personnel departments who often have savvy in this area.

So you develop the names of a few executive search firms— what's the next step? If you have not been given a specific recruiter's name, call the company and express your interest in possibly wanting to retain them to do a search. Ask to speak to the partner or officer who manages the functional area that interests you or to the senior partner, in the absence of a specialist. Assuming you have called a major bracket outfit and therefore their professionalism can probably be assured, their fees will be in the 30 to 35 percent range. Your initial key question is whether they, and in particular the individual to whom you are speaking, have done successful searches for quality companies in the discipline that is your need. If they have, and can readily discuss some, and you initially feel comfortable with this person, or another whom you may later be referred to because of his expertise in your field, then visiting with him is the logical next step. You can invite executive search people to your company or visit them at theirs if you prefer—it's free, and in keeping with the way they operate. Your numerous questions will be answered then.

If you prefer to spend more time on the telephone having your questions answered or to have literature sent explaining their services, this is also acceptable. Naturally, if the firm isn't conversant in your area, you may not care to proceed with them unless you have heard excellent reports about their abilities in general.

## WHAT QUESTIONS SHOULD YOU CONSIDER OR DIRECTLY ASK WHEN INTERVIEWING A SEARCH FIRM?

### Do they create a positive first impression?

You may be visited by one or two headhunters. They should look and act professionally. They should be well dressed and groomed, and cordial with a manner that puts one at ease.

### Are they articulate?

A firm command of the language of your field is desirable and naturally a well-spoken recruiter is more likely to effectively present your needs to potential candidates and pique their interest in exploring the situation.

### What are the history and background of the firm and its people?

How long has the company been in business? How many offices and employees do they have? Are offices in locations that are relevant to your needs? What are the educational levels and work experiences of the professional staff? Do they service a few fields or many? Which? How many clients do they have? How many are top quality?

### Have they done their homework in researching your company?

Smart consultants come prepared. They have learned something about your firm and possibly even you before visiting.

### What specific searches have they done that are the same as or similar to your need?

The headhunter will have anticipated your probing him regarding this. He no doubt will be able to mention several clients, possibly by name, and then elaborate in detail about successfully completed assignments. This is clearly one of your truest measures of him. Feel free to inquire concerning any of the searches. What difficulties, if any, did they encounter? Which companies did they hunt in? What firms did the finalists come from? What were the ingredients and sizes of the compensation packages for the hired executives? What were their general observations regarding these searches?

### Can the headhunter provide references of satisfied customers?

The ultimate bottom line! He should be able to offer a few corporate client names and an appropriate senior contact whom he's done successful search work for. It may be the president, a line executive, or the personnel director.

### What companies are they blocked or prevented from hunting in because of client relationships?

If there are, for example, 15 top companies in your field and six are clients of the search firm, this may interfere with the ability to do successful work.

Taking this a step further, and it is a rare request, will they let you see a list of the companies and the target executives before they are approached? You may not need to do this, but once in a while a client may know many of these individuals—and want to eliminate some from consideration, or conversely, emphasize an interest in certain ones. It is not unusual, however, to *discuss* with a client which companies will be hunted in. Some companies ask to see this list further along in the search, particularly if there has been difficulty in generating candidates. When several fine candidates have been presented, seeing a list isn't necessary.

### How is the research conducted?

You don't want someone who merely looks in their files or runs advertisements. They may retain an outside researcher or be sophisticated enough to have an in-house operation including specially trained staff, numerous directories, networking capabilities, and even computer linkage to diverse reference services. The headhunter should be able to develop a list of target companies and executives whom he can source and screen.

### Who will actually do the assignment?

You may be impressed with the person or persons visiting you and would be comfortable having them do the search. Will they do the search or will it be downstreamed? They may direct and manage the work of others and thereby still effectively liaise with you while incorporating the additional horsepower of their staff. You may want to meet other members of the search team.

### How will the headhunter keep you informed on the progress of the search?

You want someone who will telephone you regularly (once a week or more if you prefer) and keep you updated.

A West Coast recruiter was asked to do a senior level search for a New York based company which wanted to open an office in Los Angeles. His client, the chairman, insisted that he be apprised of the search's progress—promptly at 9:00 A.M. on a daily basis. This required the headhunter to be on the telephone at 6:00 A.M. But he did so with a smile because a major assignment was being conducted.

The headhunter should also ideally be available to meet with you to discuss candidates, problems, and events. This does not mean that he must live near you. Also, the consultant should only refer executives whom he has interviewed and written resumes for—and the latter should be presented to clients prior to the candidate's visits. The headhunter should provide candidates' feedback after their meetings with you, get involved in the negotiation process with potential hires, and check references.

### How long will it take before candidates are presented; how many are typically seen; and how long will the search take to complete (for someone to be hired)?

Quality search firms can usually present a few or several candidates within three to four weeks or less. Depending on the anticipated difficulty of the search, which should be discussed with the recruiter, it can take from three to "umpteen" months.

The recruiter presented four candidates after three weeks on the assignment. During the next month, the client met with each. They were very keen on one man, but he was happy with his job and decided not to pursue the new opportunity. During the next eight months, the client wooed him—lunches, dinners, shows, two flights to their headquarters to meet senior management—before he said "I do."

**What does the search firm charge and how does it bill?**

By all means ask. Assuming a $90,000 job and a 33.33 percent fee, and thus a fee to the search firm of $30,000, a company would typically be billed $10,000 for each of the first three months. Add to the $30,000, expenses of $3,000, assuming 10 percent of the fee, bringing a monthly bill to around $11,000.

Though less frequently the case, some search firms are on a monthly retainer of X dollars, say $10,000. This figure is then deducted from the fee when and if they place someone.

Sometimes a fixed or flat fee is charged based on an assessment of the difficulty of the assignment. It usually works out to less than 33.33 percent, but only a few firms will employ it. Some search companies, however, utilize this approach with their public and education sector clients who lack the ability to pay larger fees.

**If you retain the search firm will they refrain from hunting in other divisions or departments in your company?**

If you are a billion dollar conglomerate composed, in essence, of many diverse companies, it's unlikely that you can keep a recruiter out by giving him only one assignment, particularly if it's a modest one. Awarding several searches, even if they are not in all of the different corporate entities, may keep him away, since the fees are substantial and you are both entering into a broad business relationship.

What if no additional business is offered to the recruiter and a year or two lapses? Depending on the search firm and the time frame it honors, they will no longer consider you a client after either one year (more typically) or two without an assignment. However, an ethical firm should never try to remove someone they placed.

Of note, at least one firm has emerged which purports to teach companies defense tactics to counter a search firm's advances on their executives.

**If the search firm places someone and he leaves in less
than one year, will they replace without charging an additional
fee save general expenses?**

Some firms will still do this selectively. It's an obvious advantage
to you if they will. But some fields and jobs are marked by executives not staying long (lacking company loyalty) and the trend
to change jobs more frequently is growing. So the guarantee is
dying.

**Are you personally comfortable with the consultants?**

They will be liaising with you on a regular basis. You need someone who relates well to you and vice versa.

**Can they effectively represent your organization and you
to the public?**

If you are an aggressive, young organization you may not necessarily be comfortable with a conservative older headhunter.
And, of course, the reverse may be true.

**Are they intelligent and world-wise?**

Beyond the scope of your specific needs, it is an additional plus
if your representative is intelligent and well-rounded. Granted he
will be primarily talking to executives about a position, their work
history, and qualifications. But the candidates are bright and successful people who have diverse and often broad backgrounds
and interests. A recruiter of like cut has a greater chance of developing a rapport with them—and possibly steering them your
way.

**Will the headhunter get back to you in writing?**

Assuming you are especially interested in one or two of the search
firms whom you met and you have given them information regarding yourself, your company, and the job to be filled, let them
send you a proposal letter and possibly a position specification.
It's reasonable to request this. It's important to ask it of the firm

you want. This enables you to assess how well they listen and express themselves in writing. It also serves as a clear-cut, common denominator for both of you as to the parameters of the search. It is also desirable if it includes their qualifications, an outline of how they work, and their fee and billing methods.

## LARGE VERSUS SMALL SEARCH FIRMS

What are the advantages and disadvantages of using a large versus small search firm from the perspective of the company retaining a headhunter? This will be explored by presenting the key questions one group raises in relation to the other and examining them with the client's best interest in mind.

**Is it true that in small firms the partner does the work while in large firms it's delegated to an assistant?**

There are small firms where the partner does all the work. They are either structured that way or lack the business volume to need additional staff. There are hybrids where a few very productive senior people have assistants reporting to them while others do not—but may in the future if the number of searches which they work on increases. Sometimes the assistant has a vice president title and to the corporate user of search it may seem as if the assignment isn't really being delegated or downstreamed. In fact, as in some big headhunting companies, it is being worked on by a professional team.

There are giant executive search companies where some or most of the consultants do all of the search work and there are others who have the team approach.

So the basic answer to the original question is—yes and no. But there is much to consider. Some clients prefer working with only one headhunter because they know who is doing the work and what to expect, and can avoid their search's becoming a forgotten element on a second or third party's desk. However, the team effort employing more than one person calling possible candidates, plus a researcher or two developing executives' names, greatly speeds up a search. Furthermore, the search is managed by the partner, who is your prime contact. But if he is away for any reason, you have an additional and informed liaison in his assistant or associate. Besides, associates are generally all professionals with impressive credentials. And better they diligently bang out the voluminous, repetitive cold calls to prospective executive candidates than the partner. This would be a poor use of his time. He is best off calling his contacts for leads, managing the operation, assessing people developed by his assistant (and himself), interviewing, and staying in close and less fettered touch with you.

**Don't big firms have many clients and become therefore blocked from effectively serving them because there aren't enough nonclient companies left for them to hunt in?**

Big doesn't mean too fat with clients to function effectively. It represents multiple offices around the United States and often overseas, and very often serving many of the same clients in these diverse locations. It represents much repeat business with these clients based on successful previous work. Hence, more searches are done, more staff are employed, and annual billings are greater. This kind of achievement attracts new clients and further expansion. It's an inaccuracy to categorically believe that the giant firms would take on so many clients that they subsequently had too few companies left to search in. It's a good sales pitch often leveled by smaller firms when competing with the giants for an assignment. Since small firms have fewer clients, they can call into more companies. Practically speaking, most big executive search companies leave ample room and don't develop an excessive number of client relationships in any field. They have been known to refuse work with a potentially new client because they do not want to crowd themselves in an area.

Some search firms claim they deliberately stay small to avoid being blocked. But so many are just too small for this to really be a factor. It sounds good, but a dearth of clients may represent many things: inability, inexperience in certain fields, or the current limits of the firm's wherewithal to expand due to the competition. Exploring who an executive search company's clients are in a specific field can quickly settle the issue.

### Do small firms have staff of lesser ability, background, and experience?

The officers in some small search companies hail from big ones where they were either successful or less so, from other small headhunting firms where they were either successful or less so, and from industry where they enjoyed varying degrees of achievement. There are some high quality people among them.

To join a major bracket search firm today as an officer typically requires that one be successful—in executive search with either another small or large firm or in industry. Then there is a shakeout if you aren't good. It's internally competitive. There are performance measurements in some (developed by the likes of McKinsey) that include the firm-wide dissemination of information regarding all new business developed by partners (or the lack of it), and all positions which they have filled (or failed to). Accordingly, large companies don't have much deadwood. The cream rises.

### Do small executive search firms lack sophisticated research departments?

They may have select directories and periodicals, or use an outside research service, or just go to the library.

There is no comparing them, however, to the resources which are typically available in a big search firm. Some virtually have a small business library with all of the current directories and periodicals in different fields, and even computer based hook-ups to other information sources (Dun and Bradstreet, *Wall Street Journal, New York Times,* etc.). This can naturally add speed and depth to the work. And the ability to pay attractive salaries enables hiring talented researchers.

**Since large headhunting companies have broad networks
of offices (domestic and international), can they outperform
small companies because they can look everywhere for talent
drawing on their many contacts?**

A large search company was asked to find a very senior level
executive—and given one month to do it in—prior to an important board of directors' meeting. The firm assigned several staff
members in different offices around the United States to blitz the
search in their locales. Each developed one or more possible candidates. A timely hire resulted.

If your need is for a senior executive who could be located
anywhere—in the United States or overseas—large firms can effectively network among their many clients, friends, and staff. If
your need is local, such as for an executive in the metropolitan
New York area, then small firms have a reasonable chance at
competing. Given the volume of searches done by large executive search companies, there is a good likelihood that they may
have recently completed an assignment similar to your need and
are therefore market-current regarding good people who may be
available.

**Do small firms charge smaller fees?**

As previously mentioned, fees generally range from 25 to 35
percent of the first year's total compensation, including base and
bonus, plus general expenses which amount to 10 to 15 percent
of the fee dollars. Most major firms charge 33.33 percent. Some
overseas companies charge 35 percent. Small concerns usually
charge 25 to 30 percent. But the real question is whether the
difference in fees is too small to make any bones about considering the benefits derived from using a major search company.

Some firms will offer a discount if the client hires more than
one executive of the same kind. For example, if they hire three
vice president/corporate lending officers, the first one would cost
the full fee of 33.33 percent while the second is 30 percent. A
third hire would go for 25 percent, the lowest most executive

search companies would charge. This can represent a savings though it's infrequently utilized because most search needs are individualized.

### Do small specialty firms do the best work if a company has a specialized need?

They are staffed by headhunters who come from the particular industry, and possibly assistants who do too, or they both grew up in search in this field. So they are ideal for specialized work.

But if a giant firm has a specialty desk in this discipline—and most do in all the hot jobs and fields—you have equal if not better talent servicing your needs plus all of the additional resources of a major search company.

### Can small firms guarantee a placement for one year?

This kind of service is on the wane. A few search firms (very few) still offer it on occasion. The toll in time and money of having to replace an executive without charging another fee is costly. It's naturally a bigger burden for a smaller company.

# CHAPTER 12

# For Companies Planning to Use a Search Firm— Part Two

There are several points to consider in . . .

## MAXIMIZING A WORKING RELATIONSHIP WITH A HEADHUNTER

**Don't expect the search executive to be happy with a client who has seen a dozen or more qualified candidates and is still unable to make a decision.**

The president of a regional brokerage house sought a vice president and manager for a troubled New York office. He offered an adequate, but not exciting compensation. Although his senior vice presidents were interested in some of the candidates presented, he found none suitable. Over 300 executives doing the same or a related assignment were contacted and 17 were presented. All were employed by competitors. It would be difficult to find another headhunter who would have worked this long and hard on an assignment. But he had been invited to do the search by an executive who was an old family friend, and he did not want to fail for personal reasons. Furthermore, the headhunter came from the brokerage field and knew what he was doing. The president ultimately voiced his displeasure with the search firm. "You have yet to show me a star," he said, "from one of my biggest competitors," thereby adding a previously undiscussed ingredient to the assignment. "And I also want an attractive candidate; someone who looks like a male model. . . . "

The New York branch of a medium sized international bank sought a vice president to head a team of lending officers. The recruiter presented eight candidates to the senior vice president who managed the various teams. He liked a few enough to refer them to the executive vice president who ran the bank in the United States. This gentleman originally came from one of the top few U.S. banks. He was not satisfied with any of the candidates. "They aren't the caliber I'm used to seeing." Well naturally, thought the consultant, but you're no longer flying first class. The executive vice president was used to seeing higher level people in the top bank where he had worked. No one was ever hired and the search closed, a failure. Two years later, the executive vice president was replaced.

One seemingly qualified candidate after another was presented to the company's president, but he didn't like any of them. Finally, the frustrated recruiter said, "What do you *want?*" The president pondered for a moment, "Well," he replied, "why don't you find me someone who is a former FBI agent like me."

An irregular use of search that fits into this category occurs when the supposed prospective employer may not really have an executive need. He retains an executive search firm, pays their fee, but his real intent is not known to them. He then picks the brains of the numerous candidates presented—regarding his competitors' activities. It's a relatively inexpensive way to gain first hand intelligence about the marketplace. But when the headhunter finds out, the parade stops.

Sometimes a company has an inside candidate—one of their executives—in mind for a promotion to a senior position. But they want to be thorough and see what the field has to offer before possibly upgrading the individual. They may spend $20,000 to $30,000 or more on a search only to ultimately and happily bump their employee upstairs.

**Search firms will only occasionally accommodate a client who wants to change the contract or position specification, while in the midst of a search, without starting a new assignment at a new fee.**

If a corporation wants to make an early and modest change in the search specification, it is generally not a problem. Instead of a senior vice president, director of marketing, the client now wants a vice president, assistant director of marketing. The headhunter's research is still, no doubt, reasonably viable and only a little time has been lost. He hunts in the same general market. But if the company decides it doesn't want a senior vice president, director of marketing perhaps a month into the search, and rather wants an assistant vice president, assistant operations manager . . . ouch! That's a totally different position. All the original work done by the headhunter was for naught. Yes, he was paid, but in beginning a totally new search on the old bill, he cuts his deserved profits. He does a third of a search (one month's work) and then another whole search while collecting only one fee.

**Asking a search firm to discriminate for you is irregular, but it occurs.**

If the employer doesn't want a black, Hispanic, Indian, woman, or Jew, he may find a recruiter who will play ball with him. This, of course, is never expressed in the written contract, but is a verbal agreement between them.

**If another search company had the assignment and failed, avoid duplication and wasted time by being up front with the new search firm.**

The original firm can provide a list of people approached and your new recruiter will skip this roster when making calls, so ask for the list. The original search firm may not comply, but you lose nothing by asking.

**Do not be rude to candidates or to the headhunter.**

It seems so foolishly obvious. Yet these relationships, if not peer to peer, are at the very least professional to professional—and they are occasionally and needlessly strained. This is not to suggest that a corporation can't express displeasure with its search firm's possible lack of performance. However, the client must recognize it is difficult for a headhunter to respond in kind when the shoe is deservedly on the other foot. In any case, do avoid the following.

The general manager of a major company's key division saw all finalist executive candidates. He also turned off half of them causing the recruiter undue stress—he had to find a way to reinterest them in the job. One offended party aptly described the guy. "He is an officious, cigar smoking, surly son-of-a-bitch."

---

Another senior manager began his interviews by asking all candidates, "Why are you looking for another job?" His subsequent questions and abrasive style caused all the interviews to proceed downhill. Of course, what he meant to ask, since the candidates were referred by a headhunter, was, "Why would you possibly consider changing your position?" One battle weary executive visited the headhunter after the interview. Smoke billowed from his ears. "You've got a problem," he said. "They couldn't pay me enough to work for that jerk." The headhunter relayed this to his human resources contact. The company subsequently counseled the man about his manner and he began to act differently.

---

Don't keep executive candidates waiting too long. If an emergency situation delays a prearranged meeting, tactfully and personally (if possible) convey this and reschedule. Otherwise, you, your company, the headhunter, and the search firm may get bad press. However, there are exceptions.

The headhunter was invited in by Henson Associates to find a senior executive. When he arrived to meet with Jim Henson and his top management, he was detained nearly a half hour . . . because they were interviewing a singing dog! (He really enjoyed the wait.)

A client told its consultant that they wanted to have the finalist candidate back to meet with their executive vice president and then with the president. These two meetings would each last one hour. The executive later reported back to the recruiter that he was upset with the way the company treated him during the visit. He had been triple teamed in what became a stress interview. The president, executive vice president, and a senior vice president met with him simultaneously. For two hours, they asked very basic, case level, and hypothetical questions. He was put off by their lack of professionalism.

Avoid numerous interruptions, be they telephone calls or people walking into your office, when conducting an interview. This is further aggravated if you speak to other parties in a foreign tongue—your guest will not feel wanted.

In an age of mergers and acquisitions, the following has happened more than once. An executive was referred to a position via a recruiter. The gentleman's prospective manager was offensive, so he did not pursue the situation. A few years later, the executive's company acquired the other one—and Mr. Rude now reported to him!

And sometimes a client or prospective client mistreats the consultant. Like the company president who called a noon meeting with his two recruiters, telling them to plan for a two hour visit. They assumed they were invited to lunch, given the hour and duration of the gathering. The meeting took place in the president's office whilst he was served a sumptuous lunch on a silver setting. His guests weren't even offered bread and water.

**Try to avoid extensive delays in returning telephone calls to your recruiter or in follow-up with candidates.**

Over a two-week period, a headhunter made four calls to his client in order to discuss important concerns of the candidates. The client didn't get back to him for a long time. He didn't even have his secretary reply to the messages that were left. When he finally did call, the key candidate in whom he was interested was no longer interested in him or his company.

Another client went on a two week vacation without alerting the headhunter. Several candidates were left hanging and two changed their minds about proceeding.

Most candidates are gainfully employed, as you know, and not looking for a job. If they feel improperly treated, they will rightfully abandon the situation.

A headhunter took an executive to lunch. They discussed potential future positions for him as well as ways in which the recruiter could assist his company. The recruiter placed three telephone calls to the executive over the next few months. None was answered. Two years later, the executive called in a flap because he was being transferred overseas; he didn't want to go, and could the headhunter help.

**Think through the details. What do you and your management want in the executive to be recruited?**

A search for a chief economist lasted over a year and many candidates were seen. The chairman wanted an outgoing person; the president didn't; and the executive vice president to whom the individual would report wanted other qualities. Eventually, a "neutral" party was surfaced and hired, but only after much time and expense.

The division manager of an international company in the United States sought an assistant. He believed the ideal candidate could come from his industry or another as long as the individual had good management ability. Furthermore, the management ability could exist in potential as opposed to the demonstrated sense. The candidate could be in general management, marketing, sales, corporate planning, operations, and so forth. He was prepared to pay $100,000, $150,000, $200,000 . . . and it would depend on the man. He would know the right person when he met him. Many executives were presented. A few were deemed "possibilities" although when flown to the overseas headquarters office for final approval, they "weren't quite right." After nine months, the search company was dropped for lack of success and another was retained. The focus of the search was made somewhat more specific, but not enough so. Five months later the project was abandoned by the client.

# A SPECIAL BOND

When the working relationship is a good one, a special bond can develop between the headhunter and client. The headhunter may lavishly entertain the client, often in the company of their spouses, and with a genuine friendship born out of a mutually successful business alliance. Luncheons, dinners, shows become the tangible expressions of their camaraderie.

An executive search company can receive resumes or occasionally counsel those client executives who have made their intention to leave known or who are being outplaced. It's an accommodation to a client. The recruiter may offer similar professional services to a client's family or friends.

And the consultant may further help his client both professionally and personally. Effectively filling his positions with talented people makes him look good, saves him precious time, and helps his company prosper. It can also provide the headhunter with lucrative repeat business. There are executive search companies working on their thirtieth, sixtieth, and even their one hundred and twentieth assignment with the same company, spanning 6, 12, and more years.

And should the executive want to leave his company, the consultant may tactfully work with him—despite the client relationship. This is done at an individual executive search consultant's discretion, by way of respect to someone with whom he may have worked closely over the years. The headhunter may be prevented from referring him to other positions, but he may bridge this by offering pertinent market information. "There's a position at X Company and Mr. Y is the contact."

---

One Christmas morning, the president of a giant U.S. company telephoned his recruiter, who had filled several senior positions for him over a period of years. Although an outside consultant, the headhunter virtually lived and breathed the company. His placements greatly contributed to the growth and continued success of the firm. "The reason I called," said the president, "was to wish you a happy holiday. And more important, to say thank you."

---

# Index